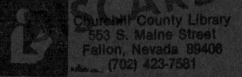

THIS FIRST EDITION OF
LESLIE MOREN: FIFTY YEARS AN ELKO COUNTY DOCTOR
IS NUMBERED AND SIGNED.
THIS IS NUMBER

LESLIE MOREN

Leslie Moren, M.D. (1954)
(*Courtesy Nevada State Medical Association*)

LESLIE MOREN

FIFTY YEARS AN ELKO COUNTY DOCTOR

Owen C. Bolstad

*University of Nevada
Oral History Program*

Publication of *Leslie Moren:*
Fifty Years an Elko County Doctor
was made possible in part by a grant from
the Great Basin History of Medicine division,
Department of Pathology,
University of Nevada School of Medicine

University of Nevada Oral History Program
Reno, Nevada 89557

Publications Staff:

Director: R. T. King
Production Manager: Helen M. Blue
Senior Text Processor: Linda J. Sommer
Text Processors:
Verne W. Foster, Ann E. Dalbec

ISBN #1-56475-353-0

Contents

Contents

PREFACE

S INCE 1965 THE University of Nevada Oral History Program (UNOHP) has produced over two hundred volumes similar to the one at hand. Following the precedent established by Allan Nevins at Columbia University in 1948 these texts are called oral histories, but that term is not clearly descriptive: brought to print, they are not oral; and while they can be powerful primary documents, as useful in historiography as the written records with which researchers customarily work, they are not in themselves history. Still, custom is a powerful force—historical and cultural documentation originating in tape-recorded interviews is almost universally labeled oral history, and our program follows that usage.

Each oral history published by the UNOHP is the product of a collaboration in which structure and content are influenced by the directed questioning of an informed, well-prepared interviewer, and the resulting transcripts are reviewed and corrected to the extent that is possible. Thus collected, oral history is a reliable source, but it is rarely error-free, as checking and verifying the accuracy of *all* of the recorded statements is impossible. Accordingly, our publications should be approached with the same caution that the prudent reader exercises when consulting government records, newspaper accounts, diaries, and other sources of historical information.

Such is the dynamic of oral history interviewing that the verbatim transcription often speaks with a voice that is almost unintelligible. Oral communication, when represented in print— stripped of gesture, inflection, tone, and other components that go unrecorded on tape, or for which there are no symbols on the keyboard—characteristically is riddled with fractured syntax, false starts, repetition, and numerous other impediments to clear understanding of its intended meaning. Therefore, since the UNOHP desires that its published work be read and understood, it does not simply bind and distribute transcriptions. With assistance from the staff of the UNOHP, Dr. Bolstad has composed *Fifty Years an Elko County Doctor* to read as a first person account by Leslie Moren. This constructed narrative, as I call it, is an effort to make the results of oral history interviewing coherent and accessible to the average reader. Admittedly, these are not Leslie Moren's words precisely as he spoke them, in the order in which he spoke them, but his speech has been recreated as faithfully as possible consistent with the aim of composing a readable volume from the elements of the interviews.

Although Dr. Moren has reviewed the finished manuscript, and affirmed in writing that it is an accurate representation of his statements, the UNOHP hopes that there will be some researchers who prefer to take their oral history straight, without the alterations that were necessary to produce this published text; they are directed to the UNOHP archives, where copies of the tapes and transcription are housed.

R. T. KING, DIRECTOR
University of Nevada Oral History Program

INTRODUCTION

I NTERVENTION BY FEDERAL and state governments, the growth of corporate practice, and astonishing technical advancements have contributed to increasing impersonalization in medical care. It was not always thus. In 1938, when Dr. Leslie Moren began practicing, the physician was a patient's friend and advisor, as well as a healer who came into the home to relieve suffering. Then, there were fewer than one hundred doctors in Nevada; today, there are over two thousand practicing in the state, and primary medical care has moved from the home and office to the clinic and the emergency room.

When I was interviewed for my state medical license in 1966, Dr. Moren was on the Nevada Board of Medical Examiners, so he was one of the first physicians I met. Soon after, I began providing pathology service to the Elko General Hospital, where Les made his daily rounds to see patients, and our common backgrounds and interests brought us close together. From Scandinavian descent, we both had lived in small

Midwestern towns, attended the University of Minnesota, and served in the 34th Infantry Division during World War II. (Dr. Moren was in the regiment's supporting artillery unit, the 125th Field Artillery, and I was in the 135th Infantry Regiment.) Later, I spent many pleasant evenings visiting with him and his charming wife, Laurena, in the comfort of their modest home.

Les Moren was born in Webster, Wisconsin, in 1914. Although his parents had little formal education, they instilled into their children a thirst for knowledge, and a sense of decency and moral responsibility. Les was a good student in high school and college, and he was accepted into the University of Minnesota School of Medicine. There, he formed friendships with classmates, brothers in Phi Sigma Rho medical fraternity, and professors, many of whom he still reveres. Les's ability to make friends is a quality obvious to anyone who has met him.

While in medical school Les served as a junior intern at Mounds Park Hospital in St. Paul, Minnesota. At the hospital he met Dr. R. P. Roantree, who practiced in Elko, and who persuaded young Dr. Moren to move to Nevada. His first few years in eastern Nevada provided Les an opportunity to work with some of the state's early physicians–including J. E. Worden, A. J. Hood, C. E. Secor, and F. M. Poulson–from whom he learned much about the art and method of medicine. (For biographical data about the many physicians whose names are mentioned in the body of the text, the reader should turn to the appendices at the back of the book. Appendix 1 contains brief profiles of those physicians about whom I could obtain some information. Appendix 2 is Dr. Moren's recollection of those Elko Clinic partners who are not discussed in the main narrative.)

In 1939 Dr. Moren married Laurena McBride, an Elko native, and just before World War II they moved to Minnesota. During the war Les volunteered for military service, and after combat duty in Italy he rejoined his family in Elko. Awed by the mountains and vast deserts, captivated by the openness and friendliness of its citizens, Dr. Moren learned to love Nevada. He was one of the founding fathers of the Elko Clinic, and served on the state board of medical examiners longer than any other member except Dr. Ken Maclean. Dr. Moren was president of the Elko County Medical Society and chief of staff of the Elko General Hospital. Active in the Nevada State Medical Association, he served as its president in 1952-1953. He was also a delegate to the American Medical Association for many years, and he was honored as the Nevada Physician of the Year for 1974.

Dr. Moren has been active in community affairs in Elko for a period spanning fifty-four years. He has served on the school board, been active in the Boy Scouts, was involved in Little League baseball, and is a long time Rotarian, as well as a member of St. Paul's Episcopal Church. Most importantly, he has been a friend and a caring physician. Although involved in a busy practice (he delivered over 5,000 babies in his career), he was never too busy to smile and exchange a pleasant greeting. For his many contributions to his community, he was honored by Elko residents who proclaimed December 22, 1973, Dr. Leslie A. Moren Day. This is the oral history of a small-town doctor whose one goal has been service to his patients and his community.

OWEN C. BOLSTAD, M.D.
Department of Pathology
University of Nevada School of Medicine

1

FAMILY AND YOUTH

MY MOTHER'S NAME WAS Jennie Mathilda Anderson. Her father, Nils Peter Anderson, came from Denmark, and her mother came from Sweden. My dad's father was named Peterson, and both he and grandmother Moren emigrated from Sweden in the 1860s or 1870s. They went to Minneapolis, where there were more Petersons than any place in the world except Stockholm. With all the Petersons living there, they had trouble getting their mail, so my grandparents changed their name to Moren. They had come from the province of Varnemo, in Sweden–he combined the *Mo* off of Varne*mo* with *ren*, from the Swedish word for clean. The Swedes still pronounce the name as "Morane" or "Morene".

I'm not sure how my maternal grandfather, Nils Anderson, got to the United States (one of my grandfathers jumped ship at the age of sixteen; maybe he's the one) but he got to St. Paul and went to work for the railroad. He was a short, balding, roly-poly man, who lived with us for the last ten years of his life. He had raised a family of five children, starting at a dollar a day digging sewers by hand in St. Paul. They had to dig them so deep that it took two crews. The lower group would shovel the dirt up to a board platform, and then the upper group would shovel the dirt from the board up to the top of the trench. He told us about one time when somebody in the lower group pulled a knife. Grandfather Anderson just took his shovel and hit the guy over the head, and then kept on shoveling! He was a powerful man, physically, but he was uneducated.

My dad, John Arthur Moren, was born up in northwestern Minnesota, near Wylie. I think he went through the fifth grade in school, and then started working for the railroad. When he was seventeen, they offered him a job as a section foreman. He said, "No, I don't want it," but he worked out a deal with the railroad, so that he was given free train transportation for going with a cattle train down to South St. Paul. He had an uncle, who was a tailor, living in Minneapolis, so he went over there and stayed with him while he attended a business school for about six months. For two bucks Dad bought a bicycle, so that he could deliver Minneapolis newspapers mornings before going to school. After that he got a job in a tin shop. One day he came home and told his aunt, "I quit."

She asked him "What are you going to do?"

He said, "I'm going to ride the streetcar to the end of the Selby-Lake streetcar line and look for a job," which is just what he did. He got off in front of a wholesale hardware company, walked in and said, "I want a job."

"What can you do?" the boss asked him.

"I can do anything," he answered.

"Well, we've got a carload of skates and a carload of sheet iron to unload. When can you start work?"

"Just as soon as I can go and get some gloves and a pair of overalls," he replied.

When he returned, they told him that they were really surprised that he'd come back. "Well, I want a job," he said, and he worked with them for a couple of years in all departments of the wholesale hardware business.

During his spare time Dad met my mother, who lived on the east side of St. Paul. Both sang in the Gustavus Adolphus Lutheran Church choir. They were married in 1912, and moved to Webster, Wisconsin, a little town in the sandy-soil country about halfway between Superior and the Twin Cities.

Dad and his partner were the seventh and eighth people to buy land in the Webster townsite. My mother used to laugh about them putting a tar-paper roof on their store in February, each of them wearing a derby hat, when it was colder than a witch's heart! Dad said his first business expense was fifty cents worth of nails.

I was born at home in Webster on January 28, 1914, the first of seven children in our family. I was a blue baby, and they put me in a box and set it on the oven door of the stove to keep me warm. One of my aunts later told me that I was there for about three or four days. Several years ago it was discovered that I had a two-leaf aortic valve, which had to be operated on, and that defective valve may have been why I was blue baby. (Nobody knew about such things in 1914.) I wasn't premature, and I am sure my mother must have been Rh positive (although that was before the Rh factor was discovered), because in 1937, when she had gallbladder surgery, she got about twenty units of blood, and she never had a reaction to any of the blood transfusions. Dr. Owen Wangensteen of Minnesota operated on her. (My mother lived until 1980.)

Dad was in the hardware and furniture business in Webster. He was also an undertaker, and he did the embalming in the days before they had a state law that required an embalmer's license. After that he had to hire an embalmer, because he never got a license. The undertaking business was tough on him: he didn't mind being in charge of a funeral, but to see young folks foolishly, needlessly killed, and that sort of thing . . . run over by a train or in a car accident . . . he was unhappy with that part of it.

They used to have an annual speed-driving contest in Webster. All of us would sit out in front of the Model T, ready to crank the car, and then Dad would crank it and get in and speed about three blocks up to the railroad. The one who got there first was the winner. Dad won that race for a couple of years. I was so proud of him! He was a speedster; he'd go forty-five miles an hour!

My father was a shrewd man, but did not have much formal education. Although he never read a book in his life, he did read daily newspapers, the hardware trade newspaper, magazines, and, I think, *Kiplinger Letters*. He was skinned a few times, but he wasn't skinned by the same people twice. Dad's lack of education wasn't due to a lack of *interest* in education. He appreciated that education was important, and he certainly imbued his children and his grandchildren with that idea. It wasn't forced upon us, but it was assumed that education was the route you were going to take, even if you didn't have any cash.

Although he was unlettered, Dad was as honest as the day is long, and I never heard him swear. If he wanted to call somebody a bad name, he'd say, "The blamed fool!" That was the *worst* thing he would call a person, you know. He had a good dose of common sense, and Mother did, too. They made do with what they had. It was a tough go financially most of the time, for money was hard to come by, but I never heard him complain.

Mother had, I think, a fifth-grade education. She was the oldest of six children, and she quit school and became an apprentice seamstress, a job that paid only three dollars a week; but she carried her lunch to work and saved her money, and after the first five weeks at work she bought an oak kitchen table for her folks. That very same table is my kitchen table here in Elko now: well-built things last a long time.

Although Mother had gone to school for only a few years, she was a voracious reader. I don't think Dad ever read a book, but mother read all the time–novels mostly, and she read the Bible a lot. She talked to us a lot about religion . . . . In fact, Dad and mother were in a group that started a church in Webster because there wasn't any church there. It is tough going to start a church from scratch, but they persevered. I remember how Dad was busy all the time, but on Sundays he'd go to church and say, "You don't send your kids to Sunday school, you *take* them to Sunday school." If he had enough money, he would buy an ice cream pie for each of us for a nickel. On a Sunday after church and Sunday school, we'd walk down the street feeling like we were kings of the hill!

I never heard a harsh word between Mother and Dad. They spent the last three years or so of their lives in a sort of nursing home setup, with both of them in the same room. Mother was dying of congestive heart failure in 1980, and had a big aortic aneurism. She was ninety years old, and Dad was ninety-three, he had lost his hearing, and his eyesight was pretty much gone. My sister and I were there when Mother died. Dad was on the other side of a dividing curtain, and the minute she died, Dad said, "She's gone." His memory was not very good, and we had to tell him again the next morning that she had died. I don't know how he knew when she died. These things I really don't understand.

We had good times, even if they were financially tough. We never had any money, but we never really felt poor. Dad built a house for us in Webster, and we moved into it in 1920. It had hardwood floors, hardwood cabinets, a full basement, a big entry way, a big living room with book cabinets, a big dining room and a den, a kitchen and a pantry, four bedrooms, and one bathroom upstairs. The whole thing cost him six thousand dollars, and it was the most beautiful house in the whole town. I visited there a couple of years ago, and I think that it's still the prettiest house in that town.

My childhood was a generally happy one, with little stress, even though I was terribly busy–while I was a kid in school, I had an outside job all of the time to earn extra money. I didn't work in Dad's store, because he couldn't afford to pay me–and that wouldn't bring any new money into the family–but I had various other jobs, like delivering milk. I also worked at selling newspapers and magazines for a while.

In 1926, my dad sold his businesses, including a garage where he had sold Model T Fords starting in about 1914, and we moved to Frederic, Wisconsin, about twenty miles south of Webster, where he bought a hardware store and a garage. That's where I went to high school. When I graduated from high school in Frederic there were sixteen graduates in my high school class–nine girls and seven boys. (One of the girls, a cute girl, had a bad heart from rheumatic fever, and I understand that she later died of subacute bacterial endocarditis. You know, it's easy to forget how helpless we were in treating so many common infections. There wasn't any effective treatment for bacterial infections caused by staphylococcus, streptococcus and pneumococcus organisms. Diseases like scarlet fever, childbed fever, blood poisoning and pneumonia were really life threatening.)

Wisconsin at that time had seventy-two counties, and Dad wanted our county to be the first county in the state to have all the dairy cattle TB tested. His interest in tuberculosis was probably due in part to his involvement with the mortuary business, as well as his activities on the school board and other community problems. The Land O' Lakes Creamery cooperative started up in that neck of the woods, and if a dairy farmer had any TB-positive cows, he couldn't use them for milk production, and he would have to take them to the slaughterhouse in South

St. Paul. One dairy farmer, Phillip Smith, came into Dad and said, "Moren, you're a bum." He told dad, "I've got thirty-two purebred Guernsey cows that are worth maybe two or three hundred bucks apiece. If they test positive, I'll only get twenty bucks each."

Dad said, "Mr. Smith, we buried one of your daughters a while ago. How do you know that she didn't have tuberculous meningitis?", which was a common diagnosis in those days. Thirty out of his thirty-two cows tested positive, so he really was wiped out as far as that herd was concerned.

Years later when my dad was down at St. Paul, he had a call from one of the hospitals. They said, "Phillip Smith is in the hospital and wants to see you," so Dad went up to see him. Mr. Smith said, "Moren, I've hated your guts all these years, but I just began to realize now that I'm getting ready to die, and I want you to know that you were right on that TB deal."

My dad always said that he had wanted to go to medical school. Dad had a cousin, Ed Moren, who was a surgeon in Minneapolis. He had gone with Litzenburg over to Vienna in 1913. One time Dad told Dr. Ed Moren, "I'd like to go to medical school."

His cousin said, "Art, you can't do it." He told Dad, "You're nineteen years old now. You haven't got any money. You have to finish high school, go to pre-med for four years, and then go to medical school for another four years, and you just can't do it."

Dad said, "You're right." So that's how come Dad never went to medical school. My dad's cousin was the only doctor in the family.

I broke my leg skiing the day after Christmas when I was about nine or ten years old. I ran into a tree, and the toe strap broke. A friend that was with me said, "Come on; get up!" but I couldn't get up. I'd get up about halfway, and I couldn't make it any further. A farmer hitched up a team of horses to a sleigh and took me into the town about four miles away. He had to carry me up the thirty-three steps to the doctor's office. I was angry because I had gotten a new pair of long johns for Christmas, and they cut the damned underwear leg to get them off me! Finally they put me on the train and took me down to St. Paul, to the old Bethesda Hospital. They gave me an anesthetic, and when I woke up, they had put a Spica cast on my leg.[†]

I wore that cast for a couple of months after they sent me back home, and I became pretty adept at dealing with it. I would rest my right leg on the bed, as I had a long cast on it, but on the left leg the cast was just around the thigh; so I could scoot over to a chair and watch the kids ice skating across the street for entertainment, until my mother caught me doing it.

When the doctor took off the cast, my leg was straight out! He said, "Bend your knee." I told him "I can't," so he sat on my foot, and I flipped right over! I remember that incident pretty well. Things were pretty primitive in those days, and I never had any more X rays after the original one while I was in the hospital. The fracture was just below the knee, and it went through the epiphysis of my right tibia (the growth center), so that my right leg is shorter than the left. That caused me to have a crooked spine; but nobody noticed that until I had my physical examination to get into medical school.

I spent one summer up at my granddad's farm in northwest Minnesota, milking cows. I learned then that I didn't want to be a farmer for the rest of my life–I milked too many cows! I didn't want to take agriculture in school, so I took Latin.

[†] A Spica cast was a heavy plaster cast which extended from around the waist to the knee on one leg, and to the foot on the fractured leg. The two legs were held apart by a bridge, usually made from a broom stick.

I went to high school from 1926 to 1930, just before the Depression started. We worked hard in high school. The principal was a good friend of my dad, and, boy, he made sure that I toed the mark! If I got out of line, I would be in deep trouble. I was a short little shrimp, and I only weighed 113 pounds, but when I was a senior in high school I played football and basketball. In those days, basketball was played with two-handed set shots, and a jump ball after every score. I remember one game where the score ended up twelve to nine! We didn't have a track team, but we had a big field for track in high school. Since nobody else wanted to run the mile, I did, but I always came in last. We ran the event along a gravel road.

I belonged to Boy Scouts, and played the cornet in the school band. I also participated in statewide extemporary speech contests. Once the principal took me down to Madison, the state capital, to enter a speech contest. They had a list of a hundred subjects, and the contestants would pick five subjects out of a hat, then make a speech about one of them. I didn't know doodley about any of the subjects that I picked out, but I finally selected Russia's Five-Year Plan and tried to marshal my thoughts into a speech. We gave our speeches in the supreme court room at the state capital. After I got through, the principal said, "You know, you must have been pretty nervous, because you said that Herbert Hoover was elected president in eighteen hundred and twenty-eight." I just completely goofed on it.

As the economy began to decline, Dad experienced tough going in his businesses. There were just Dad and one clerk in the store; but some days the total sales were under five bucks, so he couldn't really afford the clerk, because the salary for the clerk was five dollars a day. No profit there! You couldn't feed a family of seven kids on that kind of income, so Dad sold his businesses in Frederic in January of 1930, and he bought a store in St. Paul on the east side, where he and Mother had met and where she had grown up. My mother and I stayed in Frederic while I finished school, and Dad would come up to see us on weekends. He had been chairman of the school board in Frederic for many years, and after he moved to St. Paul he stayed on the school board–principally, I think, so he could come up for my graduation and hand my diploma to me. The morning after graduation, he and I got up at about three o'clock in the morning and drove down to St. Paul, so that I could start sanding the floors of the house we were moving into!

While I was in high school I had become friends with Dr. Arverson, who was a good friend of my dad. Doc Arverson had a daughter who was an eighth grader when she died of meningococcal meningitis. (I was a freshman in high school at that time.) A local chiropractor said, "If they'd have brought her to me, I would have cured her." Well, that didn't set very well with any of us.

This chiropractor had been a farmer, and he had paid two hundred and fifty bucks to go to a chiropractic school down in Davenport, Iowa. Two weeks later he came back as a Doctor of Chiropractics, and I might say that that's colored my feeling toward chiropractors ever since. I think it's an unscientific cult, basically. (The chiropractor had the first X-ray machine in Webster . . . . Well, if you've ever seen a full-body X ray, you know how useless it was! A well-trained radiologist once told me that no one would be able to make a diagnosis of anything on one of those full-body X rays.)

Dr. Arverson was a general practitioner, and a good surgeon. He had gone to Marquette University, and after I'd been practicing medicine in Elko for a while, I said to Dr. Secor, "You went to Marquette. Did you ever know Dr. R. G. Arverson?"

"Roy George Arverson? I sure did!" In the towns of Beesley and Frederic, he was the pillar of the Methodist church, you know, but Dr. Secor said, "He made his way through medical school by shooting craps. He was the best crap shooter in Marquette University!"

I had to write and tell Dr. Arverson about that. I think probably he was a role model for me.

I suppose that my respect and admiration for Dr. Arverson during childhood planted the seed for my interest in medicine, and my father's lifelong interest in medicine must have played a big part in it, and certainly the fact that my uncle Ed was a doctor had a lot of influence on me . . . but I think that my friendship with Dr. Art Johnson may have influenced my decision to go to medical school more than anything else. Art Johnson was a fairly young doctor in St. Paul who was a good family friend. He had worked in Mounds Park Hospital, the same hospital that I later worked in as a junior intern–Mounds Park had about 60 percent nervous and mental patients. Dr. Johnson went to visit a mentally disturbed patient at home one time, and the patient hit him over the head with one of those big crock pitchers. Art got a permanent hemiparesis from that injury, but he went on to work as an internist and pathologist for the Earl Clinic in St. Paul. He was a sharp man, a good friend of the family, and a good friend of mine.

My oldest sister, who is a couple of years younger than I am, went to medical school at Minnesota a couple of years after I graduated. In those days "hen" medics weren't very popular, you know, and Dad and I did everything we could to dissuade her from going to medical school, but she went anyway. She's always been a little bit upset because the boys who went to medical school in the 1940s, during the war, had their tuition and books paid for by the V-12 program, while she had to pay for everything herself! She just retired a few years ago after practicing ophthalmology in St. Paul. I would not say that Mother and Dad insisted, but it was just assumed that their kids would go to college. All of us did except for our second sister. She worked for a photographer and did painting, and she got married in 1943 at the age of twenty-five.

The next child in our family was Charles, my brother. He was accepted for medical school at Minnesota, but he came home one day and said, "Les, I don't know whether I want to take medicine." Dr. Gaylord Anderson, in the psychology department at the University of Minnesota, was just starting to do aptitude testing in those days. I told Charles, "Let's go over and talk to him." So Dr. Anderson tested my brother, and he told him, "I'm surprised that you had grades good enough to get into medical school." Dr. Anderson thought that he'd be better off in law, advertising or business. So Charles had to switch in the middle of the stream, and he went to summer school. He ended up practicing law in Seattle. However, the cases that he enjoyed the most, and was most interested in, were those related to the medical field, such as medical malpractice and that sort of thing.

The next sibling was a sister. She became a nurse and married Dr. Harold Anderson, a surgeon in Austin, Minnesota. The next one was also a sister, who started nursing school and quit to get married. The baby of the family is a boy who is fifteen years younger than I am. He went to college, and then worked with dad in the hardware store in St. Paul for about ten years. One day he came home and said, "Dad, I'm going to go to a seminary and become a minister." Well, Dad and I tried to talk him out of it, but we were not successful. He went on to the Lutheran Seminary in Rock Island, Illinois, and became a minister. His first call was down to Roseville, California, just above Sacramento. Then he was called to a church in Inglewood, California. He's been in Davis, California, now for about ten or fifteen years, and he's still a minister. He has gotten a master's degree in order to qualify for counseling.

During the summers after high school, I had various jobs in Wisconsin and Minnesota. One was driving a taxi in St. Paul, but I couldn't make a living doing that. Then in 1932, I sold magazines across Wisconsin. It was a high-pressure job, and a guy certainly couldn't make a living doing that, either. There were four of us in the magazine sales crew, and we lived on a dollar a day. I think a room for the four of us fellows was twenty-five cents a night, and the breakfast and the lunch were twenty-five cents for each meal. We splurged for thirty-five or even fifty cents for supper at night. We never had any money, but we never felt poor. I'm glad that I lived through the Depression, from the standpoint of realizing full force that dollars don't grow on trees.

2

TRAINING

I STARTED PRE-MED TRAINING at the University of Minnesota in 1930. Most of the time I was taking eighteen or twenty credit hours of combined pre-medical school courses every quarter. I'd also work some weekends in my dad's store, and I had a job slinging hash. Earning a medical degree was a seven-year deal in those days–and instead of the four years of pre-med that is customary today, I had three years, which meant that I had a chance to take only two elective courses. For one of them I took modern world history from Guy Stanton Ford, who later became president of the university, and the other elective course I took was abnormal psychology. I worked my socks off to do well, and I got good grades–better grades than I did later in medical school.

I was good in math, and we had to take geometry, trigonometry, physics . . . . We were taking a final examination in math one quarter, and I finished the test early, so I handed in my paper. Our instructor was part Indian, a lovely lady–she asked me "What's wrong? Have you checked your answers?"

I said, "I have checked them."

A while later I had to go back to that classroom, because I was waiting for one of my classmates, and she met me at the door. She had corrected my paper, and she said, "You dummy! You only got 183 out of 185!" I had forgotten to put the decimal point in the wrong place, or something like that.

I still can do well with figures, but I can't remember trigonometry or any of that. We had logarithm books, but I can't even define what a logarithm is now. Slide rules scared the daylights out of me, and I never did learn how to use one.

I liked English. An English teacher, Mrs. Delaplane, helped me a lot. She would chide me and say, "Come on—you can do it." We had to turn in a theme every week, hand-written. If we had three errors in punctuation, spelling, or grammar, she would mark us down one grade point. The best theme I ever wrote was written on the streetcar on the way to school on the day it was due. I got an A on it, without an error in it. She complimented me on that.

I took both conversational German and medical German. I worked my tail off in German, and I could speak, read, write and understand German after a couple of years. Our first professor was Herr Josef Meidt. (This was about the time Hitler was coming into power.) I think we used to meet five hours a week—on Monday, Wednesday, Thursday, Friday, and Saturday. On the first class on the first day of school, Herr Meidt said, "Our next class will be on Wednesday. These are the two textbooks you're supposed to buy." We were supposed to understand the first fifteen pages of each book by Wednesday. When I came to school on Wednesday night, after he took roll, he says, "Herr Moren, recite the Cherman Alphabet."

I began "Ah, Bay, Cay . . . . "

"You didn't *study*. Next, please," he said. Boy, I had to work my socks off for him.

In Chemistry we had Herr Glocker, another German instructor. We studied inorganic chemistry, both qualitative and quantitative, but we were just punk freshmen for a couple of weeks. After class, I went to Dr. Glocker and told him, "I have an idea for perpetual motion."

"Ja, Ja, Vas ist?" he answered.

"Well," I told him, "You draw a line with a fulcrum in the center, with a 9 on one end and a 6 on the other. Pretty soon the 9 will be heavier and pull the 6 over, and on and on."

"Ach! Some kids never grow up," he said. But after that he took an interest in me, and he kept tabs on me pretty well. He would point out my mistakes and help me out. In chemistry I did very well, but it was hard for me, because I had never had any exposure to chemistry in high school, so it was an entirely new language to me. What were there then, ninety-five elements in the Periodic Table of Elements? Now I think there are almost three hundred. I'm sure I don't know. All those isotopes and things.

Once I got a new pair of shoes, and in chemistry lab I mixed some sulfuric and hydrochloric acids together, and they bubbled over and spotted the toes of my brand-new shoes . . . just ate into them, you know. My folks were really unhappy! It didn't mean I'd give up the shoes; I had to wear them until they wore out. We used to get those glue-on half soles for ten cents. When you'd get a hole in your soles, you'd glue them on. They were made out of natural rubber, and they'd mark up the floor.

After my freshman year at Minnesota, I went to apply for a summer job at Western Electric, and talked to Mr. Campbell, the office manager. I said, "What job can you give me? I can do anything."

He said, "I don't want to hire you if you're just going to work for the summer."

I said, "Mr. Campbell, if I can save up enough money, I'm going back to school; if I can't, I won't be able to go back."

"Well, that's fair enough," he said, so I got the job for eighteen bucks a week. I'd walk four miles to save a nickel's carfare in the morning, and walk four miles home and save another nickel's carfare, and I saved every dime that I could, and I went back to school in the fall. (I would tell my kids about that, and they couldn't believe that anybody would walk four miles just to save a nickel.)

Every once in a while I'd get a chance to work in the evening until maybe ten o'clock—we got seventy-five cents extra for working at night. Maybe then I'd take the streetcar home and stop at the White Castle for a nickel hamburger and a glass of milk. That was only ten cents, and the streetcar ride was only a nickel, so I would still make sixty cents extra. And, oh, if you'd lose a dime on the sidewalk, you'd really get on your hands and knees to look for it!

I started medical school at the University of Minnesota in 1933, and finished in 1937. There was never had any doubt about me getting in, because I had good grades, but I never appeared before an admissions committee. If I had had to do that, I think I'd have frozen up; they'd have scared the daylights out of me.

I stayed in the Phi Rho house for the first couple of years, and I got lunch there free because I was their treasurer.[†] It was a good organization to be in at that time. When they had to admit women to the fraternity, I was madder than seven hundred bucks, and I haven't completely gotten over it yet.

Comprehensive exams were given at the end of each year of medical school, and they were always a bear cat! Didn't have an exam all year long, and then you had two weeks to study and then two weeks of exams. Here you are, under this tremendous pressure . . . pass or fail. And as time went on, your future depended on those grades—what internship you had a chance to apply for . . . all these things depended completely on those

---

[†] Phi Rho Sigma, a national medical fraternity.

grades. Everybody lost weight in that month, because you didn't know whether you were studying the right thing or not.

I remember underlining the books with red, green, yellow, and orange crayon–Spalteholtz (the anatomy text) and Jackson's anatomy book. Bodansky's textbook for chemistry was just a can of worms for me. I never could learn Krebs cycle, but I could draw the cranial nerves in the neck and coming out of the spine, and then just distributing all over. In the neck they come all together, and then they diverge. I could draw that (we had to!) but I always had troubles with the spinal nerves, the afferent and efferent nerves. I think I understood the gastrointestinal tract pretty well, and the reproductive anatomy fairly well, but I don't think I was really too sharp on the pulmonary anatomy. I certainly wasn't very sharp on the brain anatomy. But I did learn all of the cranial nerves: "On Old Olympus Towering Top . . . ."[†]

We had two guys to a study room in Phi Rho, and a dormitory with double bunks for sleeping. That fraternity was good for me. There was a dog lab up on the forth floor of Millard Hall, which was just across the street from the fraternity house. The dogs were always barking like mad, and the noise made it hard to concentrate on studies. One guy, Bruce Cameron (one of a set of twins from Ohio), was studying for comprehensive exams one spring, and the dogs were barking. Finally, Bruce opened the front door of the fraternity house and yelled, "Shut up, damn you!" For about five minutes the dogs didn't utter a sound. So I said, "We have to keep this guy around here to keep the dogs quiet." The quiet didn't last very long, though.

Of all of my experiences in medical school, I think probably my membership in Phi Rho fraternity was the most enjoyable. We had good food and good friendship, and I think that was

---

[†] The beginning of an age-old mnemonic developed to assist medical students in memorizing the twelve cranial nerves.

probably the most warm friendship I can imagine. We all helped everybody get through, you know. The fraternity was small enough so that everybody knew everybody else (we didn't know *everything* about everyone, though), and the upperclassmen would push you with your studies: "Come on, you've got to do it." They didn't want the grade point average of the fraternity to go down.

In that group of Phi Rhos, which was a small group, there hasn't been a single divorce in the bunch that I know about. Marriage was a commitment! We didn't get married like you were going to buy a new pair of shoes. I've thought of that many, many times.

The biggest tuition I ever paid in medical school was seventy-five dollars a quarter: two hundred and twenty-five dollars a year. At that time, seventy-five bucks was awfully hard to come by in cash, but I the job of Phi Rho House treasurer, so I got my meals and my room there. I also worked at Ann Unger's tea room, and got a job working for Dr. Cecil James Watson. Dr. Watson was working on the metabolism of coporphyrin . . . the porphyrins. That job was the best one on campus, because I could work up to three hours a day, and my pay was forty-five cents an hour. (I really couldn't afford to spend three hours a day away from my studies, but I needed the money.)

My job was to pick up fifty pounds of bowel movements from various nursing stations in the hospital. Then I was supposed to get the ether-extractable fraction out of the stools, using a mortar and pestle under the exhaust vent. After a year of collection and extractions, Dr. Watson got about enough coporphyrin to put on his little fingernail! It was a good experience for me, because Dr. Watson took an interest in me. He would tell me, "Come on, you can do it, you can do it."

Dad gave me some financial help in school, but not very much. Every once in a while he would come down and maybe give me four or five dollars. I was smoking cigarettes at that time, so I'd buy three packs for everyone I had borrowed from. At ten cents a pack, it got expensive, you know!

In medical school we took the usual subjects . . . anatomy, chemistry. Maclendon was our chemistry prof. He was a good chemist and a good chemistry teacher, and he gave the most interesting lectures we had. When we had our twenty-fifth anniversary, a bunch of us said, "Who was the best prof we had?" Well, that depended on what the fellow was interested in—whether it was medicine, surgery, or whatever. Dr. Owen Wangensteen was very good . . . slow talker and really a slow surgeon, but philosophically he was a great man. He was the first full-time chief of surgery at Minnesota, when he was thirty-two years old. Boy, he had to break down a lot of the town-gown syndrome.[†] He was a genius . . . oh, yes! He invented the Wangensteen tube.[‡] Why somebody hadn't thought of that before then, I don't know.

I remember Dr. Wangensteen talking about how he devised a closed operation for carcinoma of the stomach, where he removed the entire stomach, a little of the esophagus, and little bit of duodenum without ever exposing it to the peritoneal cavity. He had three deaths out of thirty-three operations, but when he was lecturing about it, he said, "If I had recorded only the first thirty cases," he says, "we had a one hundred percent operative success—no operative mortality." The next three patients died. The first one of those was Mr. Sandell, whose son, Sammy, was in our medical school. Dr. Wangensteen said, "Now,

---

[†] Rivalry and friction which often occurs between the academic staff and practicing physicians in a city.

[‡] The Wangensteen tube was a simple rubber tube device which was placed in a patient's stomach or small intestine to decompress post-operative distension caused by ileus, or inactivity of the bowel.

remember that when you're reading papers: what were they reporting?"

Dr. George Fahr was one of my instructors at the university. I remember him discussing the intraluminal pressure of the rectum prior to a bowel movement. It was sort of humorous; I was impressed. I had Tommy Bell in pathology. He was sharp as can be, and very knowledgeable, but he was never too busy to answer a question. Dr. Jackson taught anatomy. And who was that guy who taught embryology? He could draw with both hands, and we'd team up during his lectures—one guy'd draw his pictures, and the other guy would take down his lecture notes. We'd have to trade them to one another after the lectures. That was before copiers, and we had to copy everything by hand, you know.

Leonard Lang was one of my instructors in obstetrics. (I was pretty much scared of obstetrics, thinking of the complications.) Dr. Litzenberg was also one of our obstetrics instructors. During my first lecture in obstetrics, Litzenberg stood down there looking at the class roll. "Oh, such and such; was your dad so and so?" He came to my name and asked, "Was your dad Ed Moren?"

I said, "Yes . . . . I mean no!"

It's a wise man who knows his old man, isn't it? I went down and told him afterwards that Dr. Ed was my dad's cousin. (He and Litzenberg went to Vienna together in 1913 or 1914 to study obstetrics, for that was the only place they could get postgraduate education in those days. Litzenberg once told about the first time he charged $1,000 for an obstetrical case—that was a pile of money in those days.)

Dr. William Payton was chief of neurosurgery, and the head of the neurology department was Dr. A.B. Baker. Some of the people in my class thought that he was the best instructor we had, but I never felt any kinship toward him at all. But, you know, thinking back, I really didn't evaluate the instructors very well. They were there, and I had to put up with them. I didn't communicate very well with many of them, but most of them were good. Our freshman anatomy prosector would go down to the Harvard Bar to drink his lunch, you know. Lackadaisical, very nice. He really wasn't a good instructor, but you were told if you were doing something wrong in anatomy.

Dr. Frank Birch was the head of ophthalmology, but we had combined eye, ear, nose, and throat service, so we didn't get much ophthalmology . . . maybe just a few lectures. Dr. Birch had skin grafts on the dorsum of his fingers, from carcinoma due to X-ray exposure. He never wore gloves when he operated, because he didn't have very good tactile sensation, you know. He was a patient, good physician.

Considering what little our teachers had to work with, and how well they did, we owe debts of gratitude that we can't repay, ever. Think of the Department of Surgery at Minnesota, and Wangensteen's management of it: think of the world-famous surgeons who came out of there–the Lilleheis, Dick DeWall, and Christian Barnard learned surgery there, and the guy down at Stanford that trained partly under Wangensteen. At the fiftieth anniversary of the Nevada Medical Society I was back in Minnesota celebrating the hundredth anniversary of the Minnesota Medical Association, and Wangensteen gave one of the papers. He was slow-speaking, pedantic, boring, unless you wanted to listen to it. But he was talking about how much surgery had improved–appendicitis . . . you rarely have a death now. The thing that we hadn't improved at that time was the treatment of massive GI bleeding. Mortality was damn near the same as it had been all these years.

Dr. Rasmussen taught neuroanatomy. One of our classmates, Al Neilsen (who after the war practiced down in Northfield, Minnesota, and died of a coronary a couple of years later), missed some of the lectures. He had been deer hunting and got caught in a snowstorm, and he couldn't get back in time for class. Once when Al was sitting in one of those high chairs in the lecture hall, he went to sleep (he was going with a nurse who later became his wife) and fell off the chair. By God, he flunked the course, and had to take it over in the summer! It took him a year longer to finish medical school than the rest of us.

In physiology, the second year, was Dr. Maurice Visscher. He was there a long time, and he was a world-renowned physiologist. Old "Spit in the Sink" Brown taught us pharmacology; boy, was he a dull lecturer! A few years ago I found some of my old pharmacology notes where my writing had trailed down in a scribble. Johnny Cowan, who sat next to me, had written an X there: "X marks the spot where Les, the G.D. fool, went to sleep."

Johnny Cowan later joined the United States Navy, and was in Pearl Harbor on the day it was bombed. After the war he worked for the AMA as an advisor for a Vietnamese medical school. He is in Michigan now, where he has been working as a consultant in industrial medicine. And Wesley Spink, the fellow who was world-famous in *Brucellosis*, came there while I was there.

Eddie Flink was one of our classmates. He was the first guy I knew who had straight As all through medical school–nothing less than an A. He ended up as head of the department of medicine at West by-God Virginia. When he went there, he was the entire department of medicine: he didn't have any interns or residents or laboratory or anything. Oh, he was it–and he worked his socks off!

Lyle Hay was in our class. He became the surgeons' surgeon in Minneapolis. He retired a few years ago after he got sued for malpractice, which was no more his fault than the man in the moon, but the court judgment was against him, so he said, "The heck with them," and he just retired. He was chief of surgery at the VA in Minneapolis. He's an interesting guy. His wife Midge had a daughter, who right after the war was the first person ever treated with chemotherapy for leukemia at the University of Minnesota. She died in spite of the treatment. (I think they used methotrexate.) Lyle and Midge had two other children, both wheelchair-bound with multiple sclerosis. Midge has internal hydrocephalus—sort of like Alzheimer's in a way, you know—and Lyle has carcinoma of the prostate. I've never heard him complain. I think that he is one of the saints of this world.

Emil Holmstrom was also one of our classmates. He later became head of Obstetrics and Gynecology at the University of Utah. He was murdered by his adopted son after he went down to southern California. Bill Fitzsimmons, the guy I roomed with at Anker Hospital in St. Paul during my internship, had taken his pre-med at Macalester College. He practiced medicine up in Brainerd, Minnesota, after he graduated. Fitzsimmons died of a massive stroke several years ago.

One guy who graduated a couple of years ahead of me was Hank Scheie, who lived at Dean Lyons's home. (Lyons was the medical school dean.) Hank lived in the basement, and his last year in medical school he had a job dispensing glasses at the student health service. The dean got him a straight eye internship with the famous Dr. Adler in Philadelphia. Hank went there and he stayed on.

Hank served in the China-Burma-India theater during the war, and he once took care of Lord Louis Mountbatten, who came in with a corneal scratch that had become infected. Hank put him in the hospital, and Mountbatten had been there about two or three days when he said, "Dr. Scheie, I am going to leave."

Hank said, "No, you are not ready yet."

"I am leading my outfit out tonight," Lord Mountbatten said.

Hank told him, "You can't."

The Field Marshal said, "Oh yes, I can," and he left. Hank showed me a letter he got from Lord Mountbatten later, thanking him for taking care of his eyes.

Hank Scheie and Jim Greear from Reno were the role models for the movie made after World War II of the two eye doctors who had taken care of veterans who were blinded in the war. I was back in Atlantic City for the AMA meeting in 1947,

I think, and Hank invited me to go out to dinner with them. He called just shortly before we were to go out, and said, "Come on over. I've got to enucleate an eye for a melanoma, and I plan to use the cornea as a transplant." It was one of the boys that he had taken care of in the China-Burma-India Theater during the war who needed a corneal transplant. Hank examined his eye under a general anesthetic, and I went over and watched him enucleate and watched the corneal transplant. Hank said that, as far as he knew, that was the first total cornea used in a transplant in the history of ophthalmology.

Hank had clientele that came from all over the world. He built the Scheie Eye Hospital with an outfit of 400 faculty members. He had copied Wangensteen's three-legged stool approach, practicing medicine in research, teaching, and patient care. After they moved into the new hospital, I came back to visit him, and I thought we were on Candid Camera, you know–there was a complicated series of lights to tell the secretaries where he was, what he was doing, whether he needed help, or whatever. He was a good guy, but a rigorous, tough teacher because he was trained that way. Residents wouldn't pass his training program unless they were good ophthalmologists. Hank Scheie died a few months ago–he was in his eighties. I didn't find out about his death until I saw his obituary. He had described some rare corneal clouding disease, which was named the Scheie syndrome after him.

We did a six-week clerkship in our junior or senior year at Glen Lake Sanitarium. A good friend from our church at St. Paul was out there as a patient, and had to be flat on her back for nine months. My Mantoux test (a skin test for diagnosis of tuberculosis infection) turned positive after I had been out there for six weeks. Dr. Glen Moritson was out there, and he also turned positive. I think he had to be hospitalized later for pulmonary tuberculosis.

In my junior year of medical school several of us took on what they called a junior internship. As a junior intern, I was supposed to get a history on the new patients and do a limited physical exam. I went to work at Mounds Park Hospital over on the east of side of St. Paul, where I got fifteen bucks a month, plus free board and room. Fifteen bucks'd pay my streetcar fare. I'd get off at the city limits, and walk the last couple of miles down to the school in order to save the money. You just took it in stride, you know. (Dad bought me a new overcoat, which I'm sure weighed forty pounds, and was I ever glad to get it! Man! Minnesota winters . . . . You'd button up your head and your ears and your feet and hands real good.)

We were trying to learn how to diagnose tertiary syphilis. At that time they treated syphilis with fever in fever boxes, the theory being that if you could raise the patient's body temperature for a while, it would kill the spirochetes. They had these heated boxes that we would put the patient in, all except his head, and raise his temperature. We would put ice packs on their heads to keep from cooking their brains; I forget how high we would raise the body temperature.

We diagnosed syphilis with tests on the spinal fluid. Once when I was trying to do a spinal tap on a patient in one of the wards out in the hall, I just couldn't get the needle into the spinal canal. Dr. Gordon Kamman looked in and asked me, "Are you having trouble?"

"Yes," I replied.

Without a word, he reached over the patient and slipped the long spinal needle right into the patient's spinal canal, and the spinal fluid started to drip out right away. He said, "Don't worry, that could happen to anybody."

One evening one of the surgeons on the staff said, "Moren, we've got a guy with pneumonia and a mastoiditis, and I want you to give him an anesthetic." We were using Brevital, which was the predecessor to Pentothal, and was just about the first injectable anesthesia. The IV was all started, and the surgeon

·

said, "When I need more, I'll just tell you to squirt in a little bit more." After I read all of the stuff about Brevital, it scared the living daylights out of me, for the margin of safety wasn't very great. (Thinking of mastoid infections—we rarely see mastoiditis, now that we have antibiotics. Rheumatic fever was a common disease in those days, too, but I haven't seen a fresh case of rheumatic fever for ten or more years now; and I've only seen two cases of typhoid fever, and one case of diphtheria. I wonder about being able to make a diagnosis now, when those diseases are so rare that you don't even think of it.)

I went to school during a polio epidemic, so the neurology service largely consisted of polio and bacterial meningitis. Sulfanilamide came out in 1937, when I was an intern, but we didn't have any effective treatment before that—no anti-microbial; certainly no antibiotics. Blood typing was done, but we didn't know anything about the Rh factor. If there was a rouleaux formation (red blood cells lined up like a roll of coins) when we did a cross-match, we'd say that we'd better not use that blood, there is too much rouleaux formation . . . but we didn't know why.

I delivered some babies as a junior intern at Mounds Park when the doctor didn't get there in time. You had to do it; you had to catch them when the attending physician didn't get there in time, you know. The first delivery I ever saw was on a Sunday afternoon at Mounds Park. Dr. Joe King, a general practitioner, was the attending doctor on a *primigravida* forty-year old patient who had severe eclampsia. Dr. King called in Dr. Jim Swenson, who was the top OB-GYN specialist in private practice in St. Paul. Jim came up to the hospital, and he treated me like an intern, like a worm: "Come on in; we'll discuss this." I talked to him, and he said, "Well, Dr. King and I will talk some more about it," and they went away from the hospital to the corner drug store that was about fifty yards away.

I was in the delivery room when the gal began having convulsions. We were afraid of chloroform, which is not a good anesthesia for preeclampsia, and the patient delivered an anencephalic.[†] That was the first delivery I ever saw, and I didn't know what to do . . . . I just put a wet towel over the baby's face. He didn't breath very long, you know. Nowadays, you have to try to keep them alive as long as possible, even though it is a hopeless situation. But Dr. King said if you practiced obstetrics for very long, you realized that was just one of the tough cards you draw.

Because Mounds Park had nervous and mental disease patients, I saw my first suicide there. He was a Jewish boy from Minneapolis who was an excellent violinist, and he was probably schizophrenic. They didn't have anything effective to treat them with in those days. A nurse came running down the hall, saying, "Come quick!" He had taken an electric cord from a radio, tied it around his neck, looped it over a T bar and hung himself. We got him down, but all we did was try some chest compression. We should have tried mouth-to-mouth resuscitation, but we didn't know about that in those days. That made quite an impression on me. A couple of weeks later another boy about nineteen years old tried to commit suicide, but we got him down early enough. I don't know whether it was a half-hearted attempt or not, but he survived.

While I was at Mounds Park Hospital, a Mrs. Roantree was admitted as a patient. Dr. Roantree, from Elko, Nevada, brought her there to see Ernest Hammes and Gordon Kamman, who were psychiatrists. Dr. Hammes called me and said there was a doctor from Nevada bringing his wife down, and would I go down and meet him? So I did. Dr. Roantree stayed at the St. Paul Hotel a few days, and then went back to Elko. His wife was there for a couple of months, and I used to go down and visit her. It was just the right thing to do, and she was a very pleasant lady.

[†] A severe and fatal congenital deformity. The infant is born without the cerebrum, or forebrain.

In thinking of medical schools, I would say this: I don't know of any man and or woman who ever felt any shame for having gone to medical school at Minnesota. I think you could hold your head up in any group. That doesn't mean that everybody who graduated from there was the sharpest person in the world, but that wasn't the school's fault.

When I finished medical school in 1937 and started my internship, I was not sure that I was ready to start practicing medicine. But I got a lot of practical experience in the internship—much more than I had in medical school, really, although I had worked at the outpatient gynecology clinic at Minneapolis General, which was very good experience. I wish I knew now as much as I *thought* I knew when I finished my internship.

You only had to have a one-year internship to practice in those days, and mine was at Anker Hospital in St. Paul, which was the city-county hospital. (Anker Hospital has been torn down since then, and they now have the Ramsey County Medical Center in St. Paul, two central buildings farther east.) Our contract gave us a salary of nothing, divided into twelve equal monthly payments! Fortunately, the old Anker Hospital was a block from the Schmidt Brewing Company, and every once in a while we'd get invited over to have free beer. That was a humdinger! Three-point-two percent beer in those days after Prohibition. (When I came out to Elko they had six percent beer, and I didn't know about that! A couple of times I had more than I should have had.)

It was a good internship, considered one of the top ones. I think there were thirty-two of us interns in that class, and we worked our tails off. I remember we used Ivory soap to scrub our hands before surgery; then we would use half-strength tincture of iodine to dip our finger nails in before we wiped our hands and put on our rubber gloves. After the surgery, the nurse would turn the gloves inside out and blow them up, and if there was a hole in them we would patch them with a rubber patch and reuse them.

We had an OB nurse at Anker who taught us how to do an examination during labor, a rectal exam. Not vaginal exams, as we didn't have disposable sterile gloves. Miss Poppick was one of the head obstetrical nurses at Anker, and she taught me more obstetrics than anybody else ever did. I later did a lot of OB in my practice in Elko and I enjoyed it–it was fun. It's the most fun part of medicine, basically.

I enjoyed surgery, but I wasn't a good enough anatomist to be a good surgeon, and I really didn't have the money to go on after an internship. For a while I considered taking a residency in eye, ear, nose and throat . . . but I just didn't have the money. You know, I think a resident got ten dollars a month (and some didn't), and I felt that I couldn't drag on my dad anymore . . . they had other kids coming along. (When I started practicing in Elko and got $200 a month, I was surely glad to get it. In that era, none of the medical students that I ever spoke to went into medicine to make dough as far as I could detect. That was a secondary consideration. We all figured that we would have a comfortable living, but the idea of becoming a millionaire in the practice of medicine never crossed our minds. If you were a good investor and saved money you might, but you're not making it in medicine. I think that was a healthy attitude for us to grow up in. I think that may not be universally true today.)

After finishing my internship at Anker Hospital in 1938, I was going to practice over in Mondovi, Wisconsin. I'd already taken an option on an office, and I had talked to Brown and Day, the medical supply people, and they had agreed to give me credit to buy medical equipment and instruments and everything. Then I got a letter from Dr. Roantree from Elko. He wrote, "You may not remember me, but you will remember Mrs. Roantree. We'd like to invite you out to look over our practice. We'll buy you a round-trip ticket on the Overland Limited. You'll be under no obligation." Well, heck, I'd never been west of Jamestown, North Dakota, and I couldn't pass up the trip–so that's how I happened to come to Elko.

3

EARLY MEDICAL PRACTICE

I ARRIVED IN ELKO July 9, 1938, and the air was the clearest I had ever seen. As I got off the train, the conductor asked me, "How far away do you think those Ruby Mountains are?"

I replied, "Oh, three or four miles."

"You dummy," he says, "They are twenty miles away."

I stayed at the precursor of the Stockman, the Mayer Hotel, and met a lot of young people my age group, who are still some of my staunchest friends.

I had been in Elko a couple of weeks when Dr. Roantree asked me, "What do you think?" I said I'd like to stay. Dr. Roantree was on the state board of medical examiners, and when I went to get my license, Earl Creveling (an eye, ear, nose and throat specialist in Reno, who was then the president of the board) asked me, "Are you going to be practicing with Roantree?"

"Yes," I said.

"OK, here's your damned license."

(When I finished my internship, I wanted to apply for a medical license in Minnesota, which cost just twenty bucks. I didn't have the money, so I borrowed it from Dr. Larry Underhill, a classmate, who later became head of the Mayo Clinic Foundation. When I got my first paycheck in Elko I sent him twenty-two bucks, and said, "Here's ten percent interest; that's all I can afford.")

Dr. William Hood received the first medical license in Nevada. (He was in Winnemucca, I think, when the Medical Practice Act was passed in 1899.) Once somebody asked Dr. Hood, "How did you get license number one?"

He said, "Well, they had a fee of two bucks, and I think I was the only doctor in Nevada who had the two bucks." We got his original license from the family and turned it over to the state board of medical examiners as sort of a historical memento.

A couple of weeks after I arrived in Elko, I got invited to a party at one of the ranches out in the Ruby Mountains. Laurena McBride had come to the party with a man that I'd heard was engaged, so I naturally assumed that they were engaged to each other. Well, this fellow's fiancée was a schoolteacher who had gone back to Nebraska for her summer vacation, and he had just asked Laurena to come to the party as a friend; they weren't engaged at all.

A guy had to have a car to have a social life, so I went down to the Chevrolet agency and bought the biggest Chevrolet they made. It was a four-door sedan, with radio, heater and six months' insurance for $929. I paid them twenty-five bucks a month with no interest.

The first date I had with Laurena was on the Sunday of Labor Day weekend. Saturday night I had gone with friends to a card party at her house, and after the party I stayed to help fold up the card tables and put away the chairs. Laurena said, "Would you like to go to the county fair tomorrow?" I had seen harness races, but never horse races with jockeys, never pari-mutuels, so I said sure. And so we went to the fair. I bought a racing program and I saw a horse named Orinoco. I said, "Hell, I ought to bet on that horse, 'cause I've got a friend in practice in Orinoco, Minnesota." When we got to the paddock, Laurena says,"Look–that spavined old nag will never get out of the gate," so I didn't bet on him. But he won and paid twenty bucks on a two-dollar ticket! I haven't picked a winner since then.

Laurena was born in Elko County, and afterwards her mother went into what I think must have been a postpartum depression. They sent the mother down to Sparks, and she died down there at the Nevada State Hospital. When we were courting and talking about marriage, Laurena was worried that her mother's mental illness was going to be a hereditary thing, but I didn't think it was.

Laurena was raised by the McBride family, although she never was really adopted, and her younger brother was raised separately from her. Mr. McBride was a very interesting man. His wife died when Laurena was in the eighth grade, and he didn't know what to do with her, so he sent her into Salt Lake City to Rowland Hall, which was an Episcopal girls' boarding school. That was a real strict school. The girls all had to wear starched uniforms, and they couldn't go anywhere without a chaperone. That was all the education she had, but it was a good education.

I liked Laurena a lot. We went together for a few months, and then I wrote my folks and said I had met this girl and we were going to get married. A girl that Laurena had grown up with was going to have a baby, and Laurena wanted that girl to be her bridesmaid, so we had to wait until the child was born. (Her baby was born on July 4th, 1939.) After that, we set the wedding date for Laurena's birthday: September 9, 1939. She wrote to my folks, and my dad and mother and four of my siblings drove out from St. Paul to Elko. (Two of my sisters took the bus.) Laurena and I headed down to Emigrant Pass to wait, near about the time my folks might be coming through. We waited at the pass there, parked, and when my folks came I waved them down. That was the first time they met Laurena.

Laurena was such a nice person for me . . . one of the most wonderful I ever knew. She wasn't movie-doll good-looking, but I thought she got prettier the longer I knew her; she was sure a wonderful lady.

My first experience with mass casualties was on a Saturday night, August 12, 1939. I was up at Laurena's home–she was living with her sister-in-law–and we had dinner. I got a phone call from Dr. A. J. Hood: "Don't say anything now, but we understand there's been a wreck of the *City of San Francisco* west of Carlin. We're going to go down to Carlin, and then they'll take us by train to the site of the wreck, because it's inaccessible by car." The wreck happened about 9:12 p.m., Pacific time. (*Time* magazine later said it was on Sunday, October 13–they used Eastern Standard time–and I corrected them. They said, "Well, we use Eastern Standard time; we don't care about Pacific time!")

We drove down to Carlin, picked up some bamboo splints and bandages and morphine and syringes and so on, and we got to the wreck shortly after midnight. It was dark as the ace of spades, except for moonlight and starlight. The train had been going around a curve and over a bridge trestle that was maybe twenty-five or thirty feet above the water. The engine and the motor cars that had gear boxes low down skidded across the bridge, and I think one of the first cars that tumbled down into the river was the club car, which was on its side down in the creek. I went down to that car, but I couldn't get in it because it was in water; however, I saw a hand with a white sleeve floating in the water, probably a waiter from the club car. Several people in that car were killed.

Some twenty people had died at the scene of the wreck, and there were survivors and bodies on both sides of the creek. One dead woman was wearing a blue dress with white polka dots, and both her legs had been amputated at the thighs. Her body was just lying there . . . I sort of had to shudder. I went up in one car that was turned on its side, balanced precariously on top of the bridge. There was a man who had a broken clavicle, and I gave him a shot of morphine, and he asked me, "How are you going to get me down?"

I said, "I'm *not* going to get you down. I'm not sure that *I* can get down." I went on through that Pullman car, which was a tough job because it was lying on its side and everything was scattywampus. I thought I'd covered it completely, but later on I learned that a lady and her daughter were in the rear-end compartment, both dead, and I didn't even see them.

I came to one man, a Pullman porter, who had a big cut in his scalp and compound fractures of his femur and ankle. I said, "Well, I'll give you a shot of morphine."

"Oh, Doc," he said, "take care of somebody who's really hurt." He was on his second bottle of Scotch whiskey by that time.

Dr. Poulson, who was a solo practitioner in Elko at that time, and Dr. Hood and I were the only doctors at the scene of the accident. (We didn't even have an aid station there.) We had come down to the scene of the wreck from Carlin in a caboose pulled behind an engine, and that was probably the wrong car to send–after we had carried casualties from the wreck to the other, east-bound tracks, which were three or four hundred yards away, we had to lift them up the back stairs of the caboose sideways, and then make a sharp turn to get them into the back door. This was a tough thing to do, particularly on the mattresses that we used for transporting the casualties from one track to the other. We had thirty-seven injured that we put in the caboose, and only one of those died before we got to Elko . . . he had a crushing injury to his chest.

On the way back I got off at Carlin, so I beat the train into Elko. We alerted all the nurses we had, and everybody else who could help. The people of the community were just fantastic.

The engine came down to the depot in Elko with the caboose, and there were twenty volunteers there to help transport the casualties up to the hospital.

When we got the injured into the hospital, we had a vice president of Standard Oil Company lying on a mattress on the floor, and Pullman porters in the beds, because we had filled all the beds we had available. We already had somewhere over thirty patients in the hospital, and from the train wreck we got thirty-some more, which took up all the space. But we didn't lose any, except that one who died on the way in.

The Southern Pacific people really came up with a lot of help. They tried to help in any way that they could, without being officious or without interfering with what we thought we had to do. We got a call from a doctor who was visiting at the Horseshoe Ranch down by Beowawe. He said, "I'm a Southern Pacific surgeon from San Francisco. Could you use any help?" Boy, could we use help, particularly since Dr. Roantree wasn't there that day. The visiting doctor came up, and he and I didn't take off our shoes for twenty-four hours. His name was Red . . . . I can't remember his last name. He was so good to me.

Amazingly enough, I don't recall too many internal injuries like ruptured spleens, liver, perforated gut, and so on—mostly fractures and cuts, but it really strained our hospital facilities. The girl in the X-ray department that day changed the X-ray developing solution three times, because we took so many films. The nurses and security people and everybody were just wonderful. It is a real plus for patients when the whole community chips in to help, and they really did that.

A Southern Pacific Railroad doctor and an intern from Ogden came out on a train on Sunday, but they didn't stay very long and went back. They made the recommendation about one young man that we amputate his leg, and Red and I said, "Oh, we don't want to do that—with sulfa powder he will do OK." It was a compound fracture, and the next day we shipped him with most of the injured to San Francisco, to the Southern Pacific Hospital.

All of the patients were gracious and easy to get along with, except for one lady who had diabetes. She was apparently a wealthy lady–remember the *City of San Francisco* was an extra-fare train–and she was terribly concerned that they'd forget to give her her insulin when it was needed, and so on; but all the other injured were gracious. Snowy Monroe, who was the editor of the *Elko Independent,* and Chris Sheerin of the *Elko Daily Free Press,* got calls about the passengers from clear across the country. These passengers were "important" people, but we doctors wouldn't bother to answer the phone, or just didn't have time. In fact, we weren't even sure of the patients' names. I can't remember how we identified the patients, but it was a real hectic time.

The railroad said that the leading edge of one section of outside rail, on the outside curve, had been tampered with, and forced in, causing the train to derail; but there has been a big question about that with some of the experts, and a lot has been written about the wreck. The Southern Pacific people claimed that it was sabotage (they had found a red-and-black plaid wool jacket and something else at the scene), and they offered a $10,000 reward to anybody giving information leading to the arrest and conviction of the saboteur. Some writers and others have questioned that, and feel that things that happened after the wreck indicated that the railroad company was really trying to cover up. Their claim is that the train was going too fast for the curve, and it had been a little bit late leaving Elko. (Tom Hood and a friend of his came out of the theater in Elko that Saturday night, just as the train was going through. It was always a big event when the special train come through Elko, because we only got one train a day east, and one west bound. It was a beautiful train, and it went like the blazes.)

When Laurena and I were married four weeks after the accident, we went to San Francisco, and I went out to the

Southern Pacific Hospital and saw eight patients from the train
wreck, including the young man whose foot the doctors from
Ogden had recommended that we amputate. He still had his
foot; and it looked like he was going to hang onto it, too.

A year or so after the train wreck, Dr. Secor was fishing up
in Oregon, and he got to visiting with a man there who found he
was from Elko.

"Elko!" he says. "I was in that train wreck. Is that young
Swede still down there?"

Dr. Secor says, "Yes, he's still there."

The guy said, "Well, I was in that car that he came up in.
I had a fractured clavicle. I'll never forget: he told me that he
couldn't get me down, and he was not sure that *he* could get
down." This fellow was a named Disston, of the Disston Saw
Company family.

(Although at the time of the wreck I didn't feel under
undue stress, I did have a duodenal ulcer bleed in 1939. That
was after I played tennis with Newt Crumley, Alvin McFarlane,
and Alex Puccinelli. I had a stomach hemorrhage, and when I
got admitted to the hospital, they didn't do any transfusions;
didn't do any X rays, either, because they didn't have
radiologists. The next time I had a hemorrhage was 1960, and
then I had transfusions and went home. Hugh Collett and Jake
Read had to drag me out to the car to get me out there! I had
about seven pints of blood transfused before I could raise my
head off the pillow.)

In 1940 Drs. Hood and Roantree, who were partners in the
practice, still did not want anybody to work into the partnership.
I don't know why they didn't want any more partners, but maybe
they were afraid of losing control of the practice. I felt a little bit
uncomfortable with that sort of arrangement, for I didn't want to
stay on for a long time as an employee. They had treated me
fairly enough, but they wouldn't change their minds and consider
partnership; so I decided to move back to St. Paul, where most

of my friends lived, and open my own office there. Laurena had been born and raised in Elko, and she was pregnant with our first child, and she didn't want to move. She cried all the way to St. Paul.

We rented a house (I think the rent was thirty-five bucks a month) with two bedrooms, a living room, dining room, kitchen, and a garage. I opened my own office on the east side of St. Paul, on Payne Avenue, and we practically starved to death for the first few months. When you are starting a practice from scratch, the income isn't good. My total gross income for the first three months was two hundred and two dollars–I remember that. We charged three dollars for house calls; I would drive clear across St. Paul for three bucks!

When I moved back to St. Paul, Logan Levin invited me to come and help him with some of his surgery. Since mine was a solo practice, I was grateful to Dr. Levin for letting me scrub in with him every once in a while. He also did a lot of charity work, and he couldn't get the interns and residents to get up at seven o'clock in the morning. Hell, I'd get there anytime just to have something to do! I helped him do the first total gastrectomy for carcinoma that was done in St. Paul, as far as we know. During the war, he wrote me, "Old Bill died, but he didn't have recurrent carcinoma–he died of acute and chronic alcoholism."

I ran a free clinic down at Anker Hospital, a GI clinic, and I also had a free clinic at the Miller Hospital. When I started in medicine, we figured that about one third of our work was charity work, between volunteer work at the county hospital and poor patients in our private office who just couldn't afford to pay any doctor bills. (There wasn't any health insurance or Medicare in those days.) That was pretty much standard procedure with most doctors: they just didn't expect to get paid for everything they did, and somebody had to take care of the poor people too. You tell that to most young doctors nowadays, and they'd look at you with raised eyebrows. "You mean you did *that?*" That is just the way it was.

I didn't have very many paying patients, but I spent an hour every day just traveling between the hospitals—whichever hospital the patient wanted to go to, I had to get on the staff, and I was on the staffs of Bethesda, Miller, and Mounds Park Hospitals. It was actually a good experience for me, and the doctors I knew were always willing to help and advise me. I never felt any competitive spirit . . . I don't think that I posed any real financial threat to any of them.

4

ARMY DOCTOR

RIGHT AFTER PEARL HARBOR I figured that I ought to do my patriotic duty for my country, and I tried to get into the Navy medical corps. I was acceptable, except for my chest X ray, which showed a calcification measuring 2.2 centimeters in diameter. Their maximum allowable was 1.5 centimeters, so they turned me down. So I applied at the Army, and there it was the same deal. I was really down in the dumps about not being able to get into the armed services. About then Bob Quello (a medical school friend from Minnesota) called to tell me they were forming the first separate battalion of the Minnesota State Guard. The unit was supposed to train, and then it was supposed to guard the iron ore docks in Duluth and Two Harbors, and the power dam at Proctor. It would probably be called into the Army as a unit. I said to myself, "Boy, I could get in that way," so I closed my office on April 15, 1942, and joined the Guard.

We went up to Camp Ripley, the National Guard camp near Little Falls, Minnesota, and trained for a month, learning about Army rules and regulations, discipline and all that Army stuff.

When our unit moved up to Duluth, our headquarters was in a former candy factory. We sent the advanced detail up there to clean it out, and there was about a foot of caramel on the floor. (They sent in cats to catch the rats, and the rats came out carrying the cats over their shoulders!) Colonel John J. Lieb was the commanding officer. He had gone to West Point, but he got married before graduation, and they found out about it and kicked him out of West Point; but he had finished his training. He'd been in the Army, and must have been in World War I. He was a gentle, kind man, and he and I and his wife and Laurena and their daughter Helene got along well. They liked Ann, our baby daughter, who was born in January, 1941.

As far as medical work was concerned, I was about as useful as a fifth wheel–I really didn't do anything medically. We didn't have any casualties or anything like that, and nobody really got sick, so I kept busy with inspections and trying to make sure they kept the kitchen clean and washed the forks and knives, and I gave lectures on hygiene to the men. Bob Quello got into the real *Army*, probably about July of 1942, and left our outfit, which left me holding the bag as the only medical officer in the unit.

The adjutant general of Minnesota (the person in charge of the Guard) was a pompous guy, Major General Ellard Walsh. General Walsh was supposed to have trained the 34th Infantry Division down in Louisiana, but they found out he really wasn't competent. (He'd been a sergeant during World War I.) They shipped him back to Minnesota, and so he became the state adjutant general. General Walsh would come up to Duluth with some of the people from the state adjutant general's office, and I would have as little as possible to do with him.

I always felt that I was wasting my time doing nothing with that home guard unit, so I kept bugging them down at the Minneapolis office of officer procurement. "We haven't got anything yet; haven't got anything yet," they kept saying. Finally, I think it was in June of 1943, I got an airmail, special delivery letter from the office saying, "This is to inform you that you've got ten days to report for a physical exam or you'll be subject to arrest." I was infuriated by the letter, because I had been trying hard to get into the service for a couple of years; but, anyway, they finally accepted me. That's how the Army is–there is a right way, a wrong way, and the Army way!

I was first sent to a base called Carlisle Barracks in Pennsylvania for six weeks indoctrination. We called the place "coronary hill" and we had to learn to use gas masks, read maps and so on. I had had all my typhoid shots, but they had lost my records, so I had to get them done all over again, once a week for three weeks. We were supposed to be off Saturday afternoons, and I wanted to go see the Gettysburg battlefield, but I'd get a typhoid shot every Saturday morning, and I'd run a fever from the shot, and be in bed for twenty-four hours every Saturday for the first three weeks. (I did finally get to see Gettysburg.)

When we finished training I was ordered to Jefferson Barracks in St. Louis, Missouri. I was there about three weeks, and I was going to take an airplane from St. Louis to St. Paul to see Laurena before our son was born, but I got bumped off the plane in Chicago on the way to St. Paul. I finally got to St. Paul, and on the trip back I got bumped off at Chicago again. I got in to Jefferson Barracks a little bit late Monday morning and told my commanding officer that I'd been to St. Paul. "You stupid oaf! Don't you know the orders up there on the board? Nobody is suppose to travel more than fifty miles from the base without special permission!" I had read that order, but I was learning about the Army.

Then I got ordered to Warner Robbins field in Macon, Georgia, and reported in on a Saturday. The office was a long Quonset hut, with about twenty secretaries in there, all working behind their desks. When I gave them my travel orders, a lady at one of the desks says, "Oh, I just got a telegram for you." It was from my dad, informing me that our son had been born the day before. I let out a war whoop, and all the secretaries just about fell off of their chairs.

I was there maybe three or four weeks before I was ordered to Venice, Florida, scheduled to go to the Pacific theater with an Air Force support unit. I called the people in that Air Force headquarters office and asked for permission to go from Georgia to Florida by way of St. Paul, so that I could see our baby son. The adjutant, with a Tennessee drawl said, "You have to get permission up there."

I said, "Up here, they said I've got to get it from you!"

He asked, "Where do you want to go?"

I said, "St. Paul."

"Just a minute." So he yelled this down to Colonel Camby, who was also from St. Paul, and he said, "Let him go if he wants to go to St. Paul—everybody should be able to do that."

So I went by way of St. Paul, got there on a Thursday morning, and Thursday afternoon I got a telegram ordering me to report by the earliest transportation to Venice, because the senior medical officer was ill. We had arranged by then to have our son baptized in the Lutheran church in St. Paul, so I waited until after the baptism and took the train Sunday night from St. Paul to Chicago.

I got on the train, and it was oversold. There was a lady with two children who didn't have any seating space, so I got up and let her take my seat, and I sat on my duffel bag in the hallway of the car. I stood up most of the way from Chicago to Atlanta, where, behind schedule, I had missed my train to Tampa, and I had to go over to the east coast of Florida. That was my first experience with segregation of the blacks. They had black lavatories and black seating space. When I got there, I had to take a train across Florida to go to Tampa, and when I got to Tampa, nobody was there to meet me.

I didn't know where Venice was from Adam's apple, and I didn't know how to get transportation. About then a young couple stopped and said, "Where are you going, soldier?"

I said, "I am supposed to go to Venice, but I don't know how to get there, and I don't have any transportation."

"Hop in; we'll take you."

It wasn't too far, but with gas rationing any distance was a long way. They took me to the gate of the camp, and I had to fish through my valpak (officer's garment bag) to find my travel orders. I stayed there for a month or two. I still get Christmas cards from the senior medical officer, and we became very good friends with one of the supply officers there.

At the last minute, instead of going to the Pacific, they sent me up to Georgia again, preparing to go overseas. I was there for just a short while, and then went to Virginia Beach, and got on board a Liberty ship bound for Naples, Italy. (We didn't know where we were going until we got there.) That was a cold, miserable trip. It was a merchant ship, and the steward and the purser were merchant seamen. We became friends, and they were kind enough to wake me as we were going through the Straits of Gibraltar to see the difference in the color between the Mediterranean and the Atlantic Oceans.

We got on board the Liberty ship on January 30, in 1944, and we got off in Naples on March third. We spent all of February, 1944, crossing the Atlantic in a convoy with destroyer escort ships and pretty tight security. When we got to Naples, we were in the harbor for three or four days before they let us disembark.

The purser wanted to get his tonsils out, and he asked me if I'd do it. I said sure. We had to get permission from the captain of the ship, and he gave it; so, under local anesthesia, I took out his tonsils. Well, when I had agreed to do the tonsillectomy, I didn't realize that we only had two straight forceps, and not any curved forceps. I only had one syringe, and the needle wasn't very long, and it wasn't a curved needle. It took me about forty-five minutes to get the first tonsil out, and probably fifteen minutes to get the second one out. Kenny (the purser) promised to pay me or send a check to Laurena, which he never did. (After the war the steward and purser came to Elko, after I had started my office, and they borrowed two thousand bucks from me. I never saw hide nor hair of them again.)

There were four thousand American troops bivouacked at the University of Naples. Poor Italian kids would scrounge and hustle what they could from us. They were pitiful. "Hey, Joe," they would yell at us, "Cigarette, Joe? Hey, Joe–chewing gum?" Some were pimping for their sisters and mothers. They carried number ten tin cans with a hole put through each side and tied with string, to carry like a bucket. They'd take all the leftovers from your mess kit–coffee, swill, bully beef, whatever . . . . Those poor kids had swollen bellies from protein deficiency and skinny legs from malnutrition; they were awfully hungry.

We were transported by train from Naples to Bari, which is on the heel of the boot of Italy. The train had to stop to get coal every once in a while, and a lot of the troops on board would get off and fill their helmets with the local "Dago red" wine, and then get sicker than a puppy from drinking it.

When we got to Bari I reported in, and I found out that the 26th General Hospital was stationed there, too, so I called the hospital to see if Lyle Hay was there. I talked to Celia Hauge, who was the chief nurse, to find out how to get Lyle Hay on the phone. I said, "Hi, Lyle!"

He said, "Hi, Les; how are you? Glad to hear from you, because we heard that there was a convoy coming over and one of those big ships was sunk, and we were kind of hoping you weren't on that one." They were awfully good to me, and I tried to get on the staff of the 26th General, but they didn't want any general practitioners. The hospital staff was made up of hot-shot specialists from the University of Minnesota only.

I was stationed at the aid station in the replacement depot at Bari for about five or six months. It was a good aid station, including a pharmacist. The replacement depot was the staging area for the Air Force base at Foggia, up north, and we'd get train loads of air crews bound for the 15th Air Force. The trains would arrive any time of the day or night, and we would work as long as we had to, to process them.

As our commanding officer we had just gotten a new colonel who had been a line officer, and had been transferred to us because of battle fatigue. We sort of thought that he was really a quitter, you know. One day the colonel, who really was a "bird colonel", sent us orders to keep our aid station open from the hour of eight o'clock to five o'clock daily.

"Colonel," I asked him, "why?" I said, "God, a lot of the time there isn't anything going on. When the troop trains come in, we will work however long it takes."

"I don't care," he said, "you will work the prescribed hours."

Well, I got ticked off, so I wrote to the theater officer assignment chief, who was a pharmacist with the rank of colonel over in Naples. I said, "I've been here six months, and I haven't heard a gun fired in anger. I don't know what the war is all about, and I feel as useful as a fifth wheel." (I had even tried to get into the paratroopers, but they wouldn't take me because we had two children.) I asked the assignment officer, "Can't you put me some place where I might feel at least a little bit useful?" I got my new orders a couple of weeks later, which said, "Lieutenant Moren to replace Captain so-and-so of the 125th Field Artillery. That captain is now deceased." I thought "Oh boy, what did I stick my neck out for?"

When I left Bari, I took a truck up to Naples, and then took another one up to where the outfit was supposed to be, and tried to find the 125th Field Artillery. Finally I got to a field where the D battery, the supply battery, was. I went in there and asked someone about the 125th. "Good God," he said, "that's way the hell and gone out there." It was way up north of Rome someplace. "Well, I'll see if I can find you some transportation." So a jeep driver from the 125th came over and loaded my valpak and duffel bag on the jeep, and away we went.

We finally got to where the aid station was, which was in an Italian brick home—a stone house with walls about two feet thick, and a cobblestone courtyard with a wall about a foot-and-a-half high around it. I hadn't shaved now for three days, and I was filthy dirty, so I took my mirror and heated some water on the Primus stove, mounted the mirror on the rock wall, and I was shaving when the sergeant yelled at me, "Hey, you dumb ox, don't you know that out there you're under enemy observation?" Hell, I didn't know anything about that. Well, that sort of shortened me up pretty well, and I shaved indoors after that.

I'd been there a few days when we had to make a night move. The ambulance driver from our aid station was gone on a three-day pass, so it was up to me to drive the ambulance because I was the only one who had a driver's license. We had to drive blacked out (without lights), and I had taken only one two-hour lesson on night driving, and it was a dark, rainy night, and I was scared. We had to slip through a British outfit that was moving up, and we were crossing their path. One of the ammunition trucks loaded with 105-mm artillery shells tipped over, and all of the shells were scattered down a hillside. Finally we got up to where we were supposed to be on the map, so we scouted around and picked out a site for the aid station.

The next morning we found out we were still under observation. I asked the sergeant, "How do you tell the difference between an incoming and an outgoing shell?" Now, these guys had been in North Africa, Hill 609, Kasserine Pass, and Anzio. He looked at me with the greatest disdain you can imagine, and said, "I can't tell you—but once you hear it, you'll know." It didn't take very long before I could tell the difference.

Our artillery general and the colonel were both West Pointers. I hadn't met too many West Pointers at that time, and before the war I always thought that a man couldn't go to West Point without learning something about the science and art of warfare, and becoming a gentleman. Well, we had one or two West Pointers that I would never hire in civilian life. This colonel came to inspect us one time: he wanted the guys on the guns to put shells on the back side of their fox holes so they could display their toilet articles on top of them–their razors, toothbrushes, and so on. It was the most asinine, stupid thing you could imagine! They also raised Cain if our mess sergeant didn't clean all the pots and pans immediately, and I had to make sure all the cooking utensils were clean. I had to inspect them, which is a thankless job, but it had to be done. Fortunately, these guys knew more about it than I did, and we didn't have any bouts of diarrhea caused by poor sanitation.

Once our executive officer, a West Pointer who had only been with the 125th for two or three days, came in to the aid station with a scratch on his hand. He had been up on reconnaissance, jumped out of a jeep and scratched his hand on a rock. He wanted an EMT (Emergency Medical Tag), in order to make him eligible for a Purple Heart medal. I asked the sergeant about it, and, "Oh God," he said. "That's a pretty small price for a Purple Heart." So I told the major no, and I was on his blacklist forever.

We had one West Pointer, Duke, who was a fire direction officer, a captain, and he had been in charge of air defence in Iceland and Greenland before he joined our outfit. The Army brass told him that he had to place the anti-aircraft guns differently. He said, "No, sir. We have surveyed every possible site on this island, and we've got our four gun emplacements in spots where we can protect the island best." He argued with them, and he wouldn't change his mind, so they put him on the blacklist.

Duke was a West Pointer and he was still a captain, while our executive officer, who graduated from West Point after Duke did, was already a major. They sent Duke back to Command School because he had his eyes on one of the nurses that General Tate liked. So Duke wrote a letter, "Hey, it's good to be back in the States." He'd been overseas for four years by then. He said, "I hate like hell to dive behind the bushes just to dodge a WAC major!"

The people in the 125th Field Artillery battalion were very good to me. Our commanding officer was Colonel Bodey, from Duluth, a national guard colonel. He had had lots of experience, and he was kind, considerate, and knowledgeable. One time the general said, "Colonel, I want you to move your batteries up to so-and-so sector on the map."

The colonel said, "General, we can't do it; we were just up there two hours ago, and we couldn't get near it. We were under small arms and mortar fire. It's too exposed, and I won't do it."

"If you won't follow orders, I'll demote you and send you home."

"Yes, sir; when do I leave?" The general shut up. Colonel Bodey wasn't going to endanger his men foolishly.

When the push finally started across the Po Valley, the Colonel and I, together with the 109th Engineers from the 34th Infantry Division and some other artillery people, went over to the 10th Mountain Division, which was spearheading the drive. Colonel Bodey was looking at the map and getting a radio report. "Get these guys off of the mountain," he said. "They are exposed to small arms fire, and you can't have artillery effective under small arms fire." That Sunday they had twenty-two officers and men killed, because they were in an exposed position where they shouldn't have been. Those killed included a Norwegian, Torg Torkelson, who was a famous Olympic skier from the 10th Mountain Division that had trained in Colorado.

We hated to be assigned an area next to the big 155-mm guns, those "Long Toms", because that meant we were close to incoming shells, for they were prime targets for the German counter-battery fire. One night one of our guns took a near miss—maybe ten to twenty yards from the gun emplacement— which wounded some of the gun crew, so I had to go over there. It was a night when the British were on the move, so I had to walk about two miles after I went as far as the ambulance could go. (We couldn't break through the British convoy.) I was wearing shoe pacs, and my stockings slid down into my boots, and I had to pull them up; so I went behind a church to do that. A shell landed right on the road where I would have been if I'd have kept going. Boy, that was lucky! (That was one of the last times I saw our machine guns and anti-aircraft guns shooting their colored tracers. Man, that was fun to watch.)

I got over to the gun where the accident had been, and they had sand-bagged the entry to the gun emplacement at a sharp angle. One guy had a wound in his back, and we had to carry him out. It was tough to go through the sharp turns of the sandbags to the outside, because you couldn't use any lights, but we finally made it. By then the ambulance had gotten there. We took the wounded man back to the aid station, and shipped him on to the field hospital.

We had a captain from Milwaukee who developed hepatitis, and we sent him back to the field hospital. I think it was a University of Chicago field hospital–I don't remember the number–and they put him in the hospital for about ten days, and then sent him back to the outfit, with orders to put him on a fat-free diet and keep him dry and warm. Well, we were in Italian mud up to our knees, too thin to walk on, too thick to run . . . and we were supposed to keep him dry? (A diet of C-rations was not really fat free, either.) Finally I told our colonel, "He just can't hack it up here," and I recommended that we send him to an evacuation hospital.

In action, these guys in the 125th were well experienced. We had one newcomer, a captain, in a forward observation post. The Colonel asked him, "Why did you come here?"

"Colonel, I came over here to die. I got one of those Dear John letters from my wife, so I came over here to die."

And the colonel swallowed hard and said, "We'll try not to let that happen."

The captain was out as a forward observer, and the Germans were counterattacking. He kept calling in our artillery fire closer and closer to him. "God, we are getting pretty close to you!"

"I don't care; we are going to get those SOBs."

We found him dead there the next day, but we didn't know if it was our shells or the Germans that got him.

One time B Battery was in a house on a hill overlooking a ravine, on the other side of which the Germans had an 88-mm cannon in a church. They'd pull open a sliding door and lob an eighty-eight shell over every once in a while. To get to B Battery you had to crawl on your belly from the road, maybe fifty yards into the house. Well, a messenger (a boy from Duluth) crawled on the way going in, but when he started back to the jeep, he forgot and walked back. A shell hit some distance away from him, and a fragment went right through him. It killed him dead. Of course it was my job to let his family know he had died a hero's death; but it was really his own forgetfulness and unwillingness to remember what the rules were that killed him.

The mud was awful, and the rivers, of course, were too cold to bathe in. I got sick and tired of using a helmet as a wash tub. Some Indian Sikhs were assigned to us at one time, and they bathed in the river in the middle of winter, with ice floating in the water. They were still wearing their turbans, but were otherwise naked. It scared the daylights out of us.

Just before Palm Sunday in 1945, just before the big push, Ray Portilla (another officer from the 125th) and I got a weekend off. We went back to Florence to see a play that one of the USO troupes was putting on. We drove through the mud to get there, and the MPs weren't going to let us into the play because we had our fatigue uniforms on, mud and all. Ray was a major by then, and I suppose I was a captain. They finally did let us in. It was a good play, and we thoroughly enjoyed it!

We got back in the mud again, and on Palm Sunday Captain Ray Fisher of Minneapolis and I got a pass to Rome. We got in there about 0600 in the morning, and stopped at the hotel and went in. It was a 5th Army rest hotel. The sergeant at the desk said, "We can't let you use the elevators, but we have a porter here to carry your valpaks upstairs." We got up to the room, which was a big bedroom. The bathroom was probably eight feet wide and fifteen feet long, and the bathtub was six feet long and three feet deep. I said, "You mean I can have all the water I want?"

"Yep!"

Boy, I took off my clothes, and I said, "I have to leave tomorrow. Can you get this laundered, and get this outfit back to me by then?"

"Oh, *si, si!*" So I filled the tub with water and just sat there–it was about six o'clock in the morning. I left a wake-up call for nine a.m., filled the tub, and did it again. It was the most delicious bath I ever had.

We went out Palm Sunday to hear the Pope's address. We went over to St. Peter's square and saw the Pope, and went through what they let us see of St. Peter's cathedral. The square was filled with thousands of people. I was impressed.

When the push finally got going, our batteries would leapfrog to keep up with the retreating Germans. We overran a German hospital which didn't have any more petrol, and was using horse- drawn ambulances and stuff. Their pitiful condition was obvious: they were out in an open field in their white wagons, and most of their horses had been killed for food. When they stopped, we overran them and they surrendered, and we just kept going.

We came back to check out the officers, and I was one of those doing the checking. We came to a German colonel, and he had a holster on with a pistol. I said, "Give me your gun."

"No. I am not a medic. I am not going to give it to you, because I am above your rank."

"Come on, you'd better!" So he finally unbuckled the belt and gave it to me. It was a beautifully blued Luger that had never been fired, although it had a shell in the chamber and the magazine was full. (I commandeered the Luger and brought it home with me. When we came home, we were allowed to carry one gun. By then I had picked up an Army .45 automatic; I said to myself that I could always get another Army Colt .45, but I wasn't going to get another German pistol like that one, so I brought it home. The Army said they were going to X-ray our baggage, but they didn't, and I could have brought ten firearms home. I gave the Luger to my youngest uncle, who was just five years older than me. We didn't want it around our kids, for they could find it any place where we could hide it, so I gave it to my uncle, and I have not seen it since.)

During the push we were going so fast . . . . One day one of our sergeants and I went up and came to a cave on the back side of a hill, and we found a medical supply depot that had been evacuated. There were a lot of supplies in the cave. We went in there, and the sergeant looked up. "Hey, Doc," he says, "see that box of pillows? That's a booby trap. You take down that box and there is a grenade under there, and it'll explode." We got out of there awful fast. We didn't look for any souvenirs at all.

The bravery of our troops was extreme, coupled with lots of common sense. My chief driver was a red-haired boy named Green; of course we called him Red Green all the time. He had a brother who had been burned badly, and had a long rehabilitation back in the States by then. But Red, whenever we'd move into a new location, would find a place on the back side of a hill and stay with the Italians and the ducks, or whatever. You'd never see him except when they'd yell for the medics, and then he was there, Johnny-on-the-spot.

One time we had an aid station located such that, in order to get back to medical supply, we had to go around the edge of a hill. It was a curving, one-way road. Before we got to that big turn, where we'd be under German observation, we would stop the jeep and get out to make sure that the cover on the windshield was fastened and the windshield was down, and we would lift up the hood of the jeep to make sure things were running smoothly. Then we'd get back in the jeep. "You ready?"

"Yep." We'd go racing though there, and I was more scared of the driving than I was of the German eighty-eights.

We were in an area that was well mapped out by the Germans, and at night we'd go back to get supplies. We would stop before we got to every crossroad, go through the same routine, and then zip across there. We weren't exposed for two seconds, but the Germans would shoot an eighty-eight shell at just one person if they saw him.

The day after Christmas we left all the mud and ice and snow and cold. Our combat team—some engineers, our battalion, and some other outfit—had been called over to the west side of the Italian peninsula, somewhere north of Lucca, a walled city. The weather was just like Palm Beach, with oranges growing on the trees. We got called over there because every time the division that had been there heard a German shell, they'd just evacuate and leave their guns and everything else. When our men got over there it was small potatoes, because we knew how to handle it. We had no problems at all.

I set up an aid station there. Around New Year's eve I found out that they had split up the 26th General Hospital into several units, and Riley (Dr. Lyle Hay), a guy from Iowa, Art Plank, and John Earl were at Lucca. So the chief driver and I went over on New Year's eve. Riley and these three guys were playing bridge when I looked in and said hi.

Riley said, "Let me finish this hand."

Art Plank, the guy from Dubuque, had been with the 26th General during World War I, but he had to fight like a tiger to get into the Army during World War II, because he was too old. He was a bachelor and had never been married. In his tent he

had the Italians build a cement fireplace. (They had to build
three of them, because the first two smoked.) He had a shelf up
there on the fireplace. Each month he'd get a shipment of hors
d'oeuvres and all kinds of goodies from home. Finally he had to
have them change the bill of lading on the shipments, because
they said that you can't get more than five dollars a month
worth sent to each person . . . so he had stuff shipped to other
guys in the unit. He got about fifty bucks worth of stuff every
month. Well, we had Italian cognac, and with his hors d'oeuvres
you did pretty well. The Italian cognac wasn't really very good,
but when it was all you had, it was what you used.

One time we got an Australian and a New Zealander from
the replacement depot–they had been prisoners of war, but they
had been liberated. I got each of them a B-4 bag to carry their
stuff in. Well, you would think that I had given them the world.
They came over one night, each with a bottle of Johnny Walker
Red Label Scotch whiskey. I took one bottle of Scotch over to
the 26th General Hospital and tried to divide it into twelve equal
parts. The glasses that we had were cut-off wine bottles, little
glasses, big glasses . . . and just try to get an equal division with
oddball sized glasses. One guy said, "Hey Doc, I like your
cognac."

For treatment of infections we had sulfadiazine, and we
finally got penicillin late in the war, but only for hospital use.
The 26th General Hospital used penicillin to treat
gonorrhea–10,000 units intramuscular every three hours; a
painful injection–but it never got down to us. We finally got
orders that our officers had to take gamma globulin shots,
hopefully to protect them against hepatitis, because that began
to be a problem–not really epidemic, but everybody was
concerned about it.

It was just a tough time; sort of in the transitional period as
far as medicine was concerned. It was before the MASH units of
the Korean war, but certainly better than medical care in World

War I, and I think our triage was better. Our field and evacuation hospitals had better equipment, and were pretty well staffed, generally. The experience of being with an actual combat outfit was good for me. Living like we did, and traveling like we did, with night convoys and all, were unique experiences, but I really didn't have enough medicine to practice.

Our unit was south of Turin, near Milan, when the fighting ended. We heard that the German 34th Division was going to surrender to our 34th Division, so Ray Fisher and I went up there, for we thought it'd be like in World War I–like, we'd line up and they'd give up their arms. We got on a wrong road and then came a little town. "*Viva la Americana, Viva la Americana*," the natives were shouting, but that wasn't the right town, so we had to go back. We came up to another town, saw a weapons carrier, and there was a sergeant standing by it. We asked him, "When is the surrender going to take place?"

"I don't know," he said. "Look across the street there, on the second story veranda." There was a machine gun nest, manned by Germans. Well, the captain had only a Colt .45, and I didn't even have a syringe. We got out of there pretty fast.

Then we were sent to Turin, and we thought we were going to garrison there. We picked out a nice villa for the battalion headquarters, and boy, that night the Germans hit an ammunition dump! It was like Fourth of July fireworks going off for a long time. Bill Martin, who was an infantry lieutenant from the 34th Division, an Elko boy (I had taken out his appendix when I was in Elko), had been wounded, so he came up to visit me. We sat on the porch of this beautiful spot drinking Schenley's "panther urine" booze and watching this fireworks going on.

While we were stationed outside of Turin, the chaplain and I went in to Milan the day after they took down Benito Mussolini's body and that of his paramour, Clara Petacchi; they had been hanging by their heels in the filling station. We went around the corner, and here's this sign for Martells brandy. Captain Chapman said, "Oh, let's see what they've got!" We went in there . . . "*Si, si.* One bottle, ten bucks." Cap and I took it, went back to camp and sat there sipping on that bottle, solving all the problems of the world. We finally realized the bottle was empty, and we hadn't got all the problems solved, so we went for another. That second bottle cost twenty bucks!

Because I didn't have as many points as the rest of the 34th Division did, I was transferred to an outfit that was garrisoned in a province up in northeast Italy, next to the Yugoslavian border. It was made up mostly of the 88th and 85th Infantry Divisions.

The Tito jugheads, mostly young military people, served as Yugoslav soldiers. They came around to take a plebiscite in this town of Gorizia, which was about 60 percent Italian and 40 percent Yugoslav. They asked the people what they wanted to do after the war–become part of Yugoslavia or remain a part of Italy. If you said Italy, there was a gun in your guts. Well, the British General Alexander was commanding officer of the theater, and he ignored the plebiscite.

Tito had taken four thousand men out of this town of Gorizia, which had a population of maybe forty thousand. He'd taken the schoolteachers, the doctors, the lawyers, the accountants–anyone who had more than a minor education was taken to Yugoslavia, and they were never heard from again. Tito had a big fight with Mahajlovic, who was a royalist sympathizer, and later Tito, who was a communist, had him executed.

We had quite a few accidents there, mostly car accidents, a lot of crazy driving with trucks, Jeeps and weapons carriers. Then I got transferred to Leghorn on the Italian west coast, north of the Arno river. The 36th Infantry Division (from the Texas National Guard) had made first landing at Salerno, and they had spearheaded the attack across the Arno. They had lost a lot of troops during the Italian Campaign. Mark Clark, the American general, chose the 36th Division to take Leghorn. The

109th Engineers, from our 34th Division, were called in to help clean up the booby traps in Leghorn. In one square block there were about ten thousand booby traps—now that's just a lot of risk involved!

I was with a medical detachment that was supervising a German POW camp that had about five thousand prisoners. There were five concentric rings of concertina (barbed) wire around the camp, and the innermost ring held the hard-core Nazis, while the outer rings apparently held the lesser fry. There were prisoners escaping every night, and once they got out and joined the *partisani* you couldn't tell one from the other. So, without saying anything to anybody, one night when it was totally dark, the Americans brought in the 442nd Regiment (the Japanese-Americans) to guard the prisoner-of-war camp. The next morning there were three or four German bodies draped over the concertina wire. They just left them there. The escapes dropped to about zero after that night.

While I was there I got a chance to take a six-day pass up to Switzerland, so I got on the train up to Milan, and found another train into Switzerland. When I got back to Leghorn, I reported in two days late. The commanding officer said, "I'm kind of glad you're here, because you've got orders to leave in about two hours. Take the train to Naples. You are going home."

I had accumulated a bunch of stuff, you know—radios and all that sort of stuff with which I was going to make a financial killing. Well, I sold one of the radios to an officer for twenty-five dollars, and then I just gave him all the rest of the stuff, too. When we got on this train going from Leghorn to Naples, they found out I was the senior officer, so I was supposed to be the train commander. I couldn't find any other place to ride, so I was in a boxcar that was so full of men that there wasn't room for all of us to lie down at the same time. It took about three days to get to Naples; then I had to wait for ten days in the Naples replacement depot to get a transportation allotment to come home.

I came back on a U.S. Navy cruiser that had been converted to an aircraft carrier. We made it home in ten days. A little lieutenant got on board the ship in Naples harbor, and even before we sailed, he was seasick just getting on board. I had to give him IVs all the way back–he was just out of it. He had won fifteen thousand bucks in a poker game in the replacement depot, and when it was time to get off the ship after we arrived in Virginia, somebody had stolen his money. He said, "I don't care. I've just got to get off this cotton-pickin' ship!"

When we reported in in Virginia, we were given a ticket for our first cooked meal in the United States. Steak, milk, buns, et cetera . . . . I asked the sergeant, "You mean that I can have all of the milk I want?" I drank almost four quarts of milk. I couldn't eat all of my steak, but that milk tasted as good as the nectar of the gods.

I took the train from Virginia to Salt Lake City, a troop train–they had three tiers of bunks made up of iron pipes to sleep in, and it took three days to get to Salt Lake City. I reported in there early one afternoon at Fort Douglas, which was the discharge center. I told them, "My wife and two children are living in Elko; can you give me my ticket now, so that I can go right home?"

"Wait a minute. You've got to go through the seven stations." Like the seven stations of the cross, I think. They wouldn't let me go. Since I had to stay until the next day, I called Dr. Emil G. Holmstrom, who was one of my Phi Rho classmates and was head of obstetrics at Utah. He said, "Well, I'll come by and pick you up, and you'll come to my house for supper." They had their first adopted boy, who was about six months old, and it was the first time I had a held a baby for a long time . . . first time I had had a home-cooked meal in ages. Boy, was I in seventh heaven!

The next day I went through all of the stations. They asked me, "Do you want to sign this paper to stay in the reserves?"

"No! I've had enough of the military; I just want to get home!"

I got on the bus and got into Elko about midnight, debarking at the bus station down there across from the Commercial Hotel, and there wasn't a taxi or anything. I couldn't carry both my bags, so I left the big duffle bag there, carried my valpak, and walked home, which was across from where the Ranch Inn was later built. God, never was I so glad to see people in my life!

We woke up Ann, who was almost five. "Do you know who this is?"

"That's my daddy!"

She had a grip on me that darn near choked me, and she just wasn't going to let me go! Alan, the boy who was almost three, hadn't seen many men around, so it was three days before he would let me hold him. It was a wonderful homecoming.

Laurena had sold the car that we had, the Chevrolet I had gotten when I first came to Elko, because she couldn't afford to run it. I think I had kept thirty-five to forty bucks a month out of my Army paycheck for living expenses, and the rest of it had gone to Laurena on allotment. It wasn't very much, but she had managed.

Laurena had moved back to Elko in 1944. She had lived with my folks in St. Paul after I went in the Army, but their house was jammed, and she just sort of felt that she and the two children were imposing on them. Anyway, Laurena was an Elko girl, and she never was really happy living in St. Paul. Nevada was her home.

George Collett *(left)* and Leslie
Moren *(below)*, two of the
founders of the Elko Clinic, ca.
late 1940s. *(Courtesy Elko
Regional Medical Center)*

Robert Roantree (*top*) and Dale Hadfield (*bottom*), two of the founders of the Elko Clinic, ca. late 1940s. (*Courtesy Elko Regional Medical Center and Northeastern Nevada Museum, respectively*)

Arthur J. Hood, Sr. *(top)* and Charles Secor , ca. late 1940s. *(Courtesy Elko Regional Medical Center)*

Elko General Hospital, ca. 1922
(Courtesy Northeastern Nevada Museum)

(Top) Leslie Moren opened his first Elko office in 1946 in space above the Palm Saloon. *(Bottom)* The Commercial Hotel, owned and operated by Newton Crumley. *(Photos by Owen Bolstad, 1992)*

(Top) Leslie Moren by the family's summer cottage in Lamoille. (Bottom) The Moren residence in Elko. (Photos by Owen Bolstad, 1992)

5

Development of the Elko Clinic

WHEN I CAME BACK to Elko after the war, I talked to Dr. Roantree and Dr. Hood. They still weren't interested in developing a partnership arrangement, so I started my own office, which I opened in February of 1946 on Railroad Street, over the Palm Saloon. Before I opened my office I talked to a bank and told them I had to buy some equipment, and that I could get what I needed in Salt Lake City. They said to go ahead and get it, and let them know what it cost, and they would have me sign a note. I had a hard time getting a car, even a second-hand car, but finally I did.

When I opened my own office, I would make rounds at about eight o'clock in the morning to visit all of my hospitalized patients and do any assistant surgery that I might have scheduled. (While I am not a surgeon, I had to assist the other doctors with a lot of surgery.) As soon as I got done at the hospital, usually around nine-thirty or ten o'clock in the morning, I would go to the office and work all day, sometimes through the noon hour as well. I would leave around six o'clock at night, and then I would make night rounds at the hospital after office hours. It didn't make any difference whether I had been up during the night or not–you just had to do it. I didn't ordinarily go to the office on Saturdays and Sundays, but of course we still had hospital work to do on the weekends. That was unending; you never got done with that. Remember, there weren't too many doctors in town. Besides the four of us that eventually started the Elko Clinic partnership, I think there were only two other doctors in town. The only time we would take time off is when we went on vacation or to meetings.

I saw the usual sort of medical problems–routine pediatric care, prenatal and postpartum visits, hypertension, upper respiratory infections, and kidney infections. We were always busy enough, and I don't think I ever went to bed at night without wondering if I might have missed some diagnosis by forgetting to ask the right questions or failing to notice some symptom or sign. These things worry any busy doctor.

During a typical day, I suppose I saw thirty to forty patients . . . I don't know; I never kept track. I was busy all the time. It was always embarrassing, because I tried to see patients by appointments, and I often had to keep people waiting some time, particularly if I'd get called to the hospital for some emergency. In those days, of course, they didn't have emergency room physicians, so every physician was on call for emergencies. We had a fair number of accident cases, such as haying accidents, ranch accidents, and the highway accidents.

On September 5, 1946 (I remember the date, because it was my parents' wedding anniversary), a chartered Trans-Lux Douglas DC-3 that was trying to land at the Elko airport in bad weather missed its approach and crashed about two-and-one-half miles west of the airport. Twenty passengers were killed outright. One person lived long enough to get to the hospital, but he didn't survive. While we were out there at the crash scene, looking around, we heard a little cry. There was a baby lying about fifty yards away from the rest of the wreckage. All he had was a broken clavicle. Peter Link was his name, and his sister and his parents were all on board the plane and were killed. He was called a miracle child. An uncle in New York came to take care of him. There wasn't anything much that we could do for the rest of the people.

I was on call nearly every weekend. Once in a while, when I wanted to take Laurena and the kids out somewhere, I'd call Dr. Dale Hadfield. I'd say. "Are you going to be busy? We'll be gone for four or five hours."

"Fine." He was just like a brother to me, a grand man. We were close friends, and each of us trusted the other. You knew that your patient was being well cared for if you weren't there.

Dr. Paul J. Del Guidice had come to Elko in 1944. He came during the time that I was overseas, and he was working for the partnership of Roantree and Secor until 1946. After I opened my own office he decided to leave the group, and he wanted me to rent space to him in my office. I had my office upstairs over the Palm Bar, and there just wasn't enough space for him, too, so he opened up his own office and practiced there until he died.

After I started my own office, Dr. George Collett came to Elko and talked to Dr. Hadfield about getting started in the community. Hadfield came to me and wanted to know if I'd take a partner. I said, "Dale, I just opened my office, and I don't know if I can make a living or not. Why don't you go talk to the Roantree and Secor group?"

About then we started talking partnership, because we thought that we could practice better medicine if we pooled our resources. I think it was in the summer of 1947 that a fellow by the name of Galen Bell was building an office building at 946 Idaho Street; it was going to be about ninety-five hundred square feet. He was interested in leasing the ground floor, and we decided that the idea of establishing a multispeciality medical clinic in that space was a good one. We leased it on January 1, 1948, and that was the beginning of the Elko Clinic.

There were four of us–Dr. Roantree, Dr. George Collett, Dr. Dale Hadfield, and me. Drs. Secor and A. J. Hood (Tom Hood's father) were made associates, since they were close to retirement age. We had our offices upstairs in what was the First National Bank building. You had to go up a two-tiered stairway to get to the office.

A. J. Hood had come to Elko in 1903 from the University of Michigan. (There were only three trees in Elko when he got here.) He brought the first X-ray machine into this part of Nevada; and he had one finger amputated, and lots of skin cancers on his hands due to radiation from operating that old unshielded machine–they really didn't know very much about the dangers of radiation in those days.

Dr. Hood used to get cloudy films, so he had the Westinghouse people come out, and they took a look and said, "Oh, you've got to put your films in a lead container!" He had them on the floor in a cardboard box, next to the X-ray machine, and had partly exposed the film! He also got one of the first wire recorders–it was a big, cumbersome thing, and it was hard to tell if you were using it right or not, but he loved the gadget part of it.

Dr. Hood did surgery and made house calls, and the Western Pacific and Southern Pacific locomotive engineers all had instructions that if they saw him waiting alongside the tracks, they were to give him a ride whichever way he was going. Several times he took the train down to Palisades, in Carlin Canyon, and from there rode the Eureka narrow gauge railroad to some ranch. He would operate for an appendicitis, on the kitchen table at the ranch, using chloroform anesthesia, stay there a couple of days, and take the train back to Elko. We were all appointed railroad surgeons–they just paid us with passes on the railroad, and we did get some life insurance from the railroad at that time. In return, we were supposed to respond to injuries and see the railroad employees for whatever they needed.

In 1919 Dr. Hood went to the legislature and got enabling legislation passed so that Elko County could build Elko General Hospital as one of the first county hospitals in Nevada. Elko General Hospital opened in 1921, but the building was patterned after Saint Francis Hospital in San Francisco, so it was almost obsolete when it was built as far as design was concerned. It was about a fifty-bed hospital when I came to Elko, and it was pretty well equipped. (There was a lady who had a birthing home in Elko before then, and Dr. Shaw had a private hospital at the top of the hill on Court Street.)

Dr. Secor was a graduate of Marquette University in Milwaukee; then he practiced in Tuscarora and later in Cherry Creek, both in Nevada. He was sent over to France during World War I, and came back and worked with and for Hood and Roantree, but he never became a partner.

He was one of the few men I've known who would find something to laugh about almost every day. Once a fellow from Mountain City came in to see him. "Dr. Secor," he says, "one of my buddies up there has got diarrhea. He asked if you could send some medicine." So Dr. Secor ordered some medicine for him, and, as a joke, sent the cork from a wide-mouthed bottle up with him. Several days later that fellow came in and said, "Damn you! I couldn't tell whether it was the medicine or looking at that cork that cured me!"

Dr. Roantree had gone to medical school at Washington University in St. Louis; I think he took two years at Wisconsin and finished up down in St. Louis. (He had been a classmate for part of that time with Alton Ochsner, and It was through Dr. Roantree that I introduced myself to Dr. Ochsner at a meeting that we had gone to.) Dr. Roantree took a year as a surgery resident in Ogden with Dr. Doug Dumke, who was a Southern Pacific Railroad surgeon in those days, and then he came out to Elko and did general practice and surgery and traumatic orthopedics. His wife was Dr. A. J. Hood's sister-in-law, so Tom Hood was a nephew of Dr. Roantree.

Dr. Roantree was really a studious type of doctor, and he and Dr. Hood went to medical meetings all over the country. He was on the state board of medical examiners (Drs. Roantree, Hood, and Secor had all been presidents of the state medical association at some time), and he was also a member of the American College of Surgeons. (He was grandfathered in, basically, but he deserved it, because he did practice good, conservative surgery.) When Dr. Roantree died, Vail Pittman, who was then governor, appointed me to take his place on the board in 1950.

Dr. George Collett (who was a board-certified surgeon, trained in Chicago) started practicing in Elko in 1946, and he died in February of 1954 of an acute myocardial infarction. His wife called me up one night about one o'clock a.m. and said, "Les, George has got a pain between his shoulder blades."

Some symptoms are a red flag a mile high, and God, I was up there, I think, in five minutes. George says, "I didn't think coronaries would hurt this much."

And I said, "Well, maybe it's not a coronary."

He said, "Oh, bull! Nothing else could hurt this much." He said, "I'll be a damn fool, no one in my family has ever had a coronary before; and besides, there are a lot of things I want to get done yet." He was dead in about thirty minutes.

George had written an article for *The Journal of Surgery, Obstetrics and Gynecology* that was published posthumously. The thesis of his article was that a board-certified surgeon can come into a small town and not compete with the general practitioners in the town, but rather help improve the quality of medicine. I have thought so many times that he really meant that. He wasn't competing with anybody, but he was adding expertise, and a quality of care that the general practitioners could not offer. He was a very astute man—he hadn't had as much experience in traumatic orthopedics as Dr. Roantree had, but he had enough surgical sense to know what was the proper thing to do. (That was in the days before total hip replacements, and so on.)

One time we had a sailor who was traveling through Elko, who had been admitted to a Navy hospital down in the Bay area. He came in to see Dr. Collett with sort of vague pain, and not a very good history of anything. George examined him, and did a white blood cell count. His belly was tender, but the pain was not acute or in any particular place. We repeated the hemoglobin test about twelve hours later, and it had dropped a gram. George said, "I'll bet he's got a ruptured spleen," and sure enough he did. George made the diagnosis just on the basis of a drop in hemoglobin and persistent abdominal pain and discomfort. There wasn't really a very good history, but there are not too many things that will do that. I thought, "There is one smart old codger," and he was. He was a concerned physician who thought about his patients and about all the possible problems.

In some ways Dr. Collett was a lot like Dr. Owen Wangensteen at Minnesota, who was a thoughtful person who was interested in teaching his residents how to think. They could learn technique from a book, but it is hard to teach people to think. You just have to keep hammering away at them to develop a "what if" attitude. (Dr. Wangensteen was an anachronism—a farmer from northern Minnesota who went to medical school.)

When we decided to form the partnership, I gave up my old office lease and moved into the new building on January first. The other men were smarter than I was, and they didn't move in until later, when the building was finished. When I first started seeing patients there, I had to step over carpenters, plumbers, electricians and all that were still finishing up the building. I often worked in the office at night when the building was brand new. They'd used wooden beams, tying them together, and because they were still curing, they would shrink and make cracking noises that scared the daylights out of me.

We finally got started, but for the first six months none of us drew a dime, because we didn't have any backlog of accounts receivable. I had maybe four thousand bucks on the book, and I don't think I collected five dollars out of that. After about six months the net income was a little healthier, for we had all moved into the new building. Then the owner presented us with a bill for $10,000 because there was extra plumbing and electrical work that we had had to do.

We spent hours trying to decide how to best utilize that space. We weren't smart enough to find an architectural firm that dealt with clinic buildings, so we made a lot of mistakes, but it was a usable clinic. In late 1949 we purchased the building from Mr. Bell, the deal being sealed with a handshake and a one-dollar bill.

When we started the clinic, it was with the concept that even in a small town most specialty groups could practice good medicine and survive financially. For me, it was important that I didn't have to be involved in the business side of medicine. I didn't know who paid their bills, and I could care less–that was the job of the front office. We all attended "medical meetings" (now they're called CME or Continuing Medical Education) every year as part of our partnership contract. I was glad to be able to practice medicine this way, because I could get immediate consultation help, even if it was only a curbstone consultation. That acted as a stimulus for a guy to do what was right or consider what should be done next with the patient.

You could call for immediate help when you needed it, whether it was a surgical or medical problem. That was the epitome of feeling a part of practicing good medicine, and it makes you feel like you are doing a reasonably decent job. I think I made fewer mistakes because of that group arrangement than if I had been on my own. The emotional support from the partners is also a tremendous help in feeling that you are practicing good medicine.

When the clinic started we did group billing. The first year the surgeons got eight thousand dollars, while Dale and I, the general practitioners, got six thousand. At the end of that year we sat down, and Dr. Collett said, "You guys are up nights and on OBs, and you are putting in more hours than we are, and it isn't fair. Everything should be divided evenly." When we started the group, our contracts didn't get signed for a year. I guess everybody trusted everybody else. Our contract said that we had to go to medical meetings two weeks out of every year, and we always did that.

After we formed the partnership, we tried to arrange it so that somebody was always on call. If somebody was off call, he would be called only in an emergency or if they couldn't get hold of the man who was supposed to be on call. When the hospital began to employ emergency room physicians about a decade ago, it took a big load off the rest of us as far as those sorts of nuisance-type emergency room cases went. Before we had full-time ER physicians, somebody would come into the hospital with an illness or something, and you would have to leave the office to go up to see them. Now we alternate weekends on call. It is really, I think, a necessary thing for a doctor to have some time off. When I look back now at how hard I worked, I spent entirely too little time doing things with my children and my wife.

Dr. Hadfield and I did most of the obstetrics; it was just a work deal. Dr. Roantree and Dr. George Collett put in almost as many hours as we did, but they had fewer night calls because they didn't do routine obstetrics . . . and we did a fair amount of obstetrics in those days![†] In fact, when I came back after the war I told them I was going to raise my charge for an obstetrical fee clear up to seventy-five dollars, including prenatal care, delivery, post-op or postpartum care. The other doctors told me that I would never get any work to do, charging that much, but

---

[†] Dr. Moren estimates that during his medical career of some fifty-four years, he has delivered over five thousand babies.

it didn't seem to make any difference. Ever since, obstetrics was the busiest part of my practice, and it was the fun part. The numbers of dollars that are charged for obstetrics now are not relative, because of inflation. Maybe $75 then was worth as much as $750 now, I don't know, but the percentage of patients that paid their bills then is about the same as it is now, probably.

Obstetrics is fun when everything goes well. When a patient first came in with a pregnancy, we would see her every month for the first seven months. We would see her every two weeks in the eighth month, and every week in the last month of pregnancy. We would check her weight and blood pressure, and test her urine. If there was any sign of urinary tract infection, we would get a clean mid-stream urine specimen to examine. We seldom would catheterize a female patient, because it usually isn't necessary, and catheterization is not without some risk in itself. In the early days we would treat a urinary infection with sulfa drugs, which were reasonably effective. Later we got penicillin and other useful antibiotics to use for infections.

We had generally good laboratory technicians to help us, but not many techs in the early days were as well trained as they are now. Some of them were nurses that just sort of picked up on the laboratory work. Of course, that was in the days before amniocentesis. We didn't do very many X rays, because we recognized that X rays could be harmful; and we didn't have automated counters, and had to count blood cells manually in those old counting chambers. We didn't know anything about cortisol or cortisol production. Bacteriology was really fairly crude, and we didn't do much sensitivity testing, because we didn't have any antibiotics to test sensitivity to! We certainly did not overutilize the laboratory, and a lot of the time I don't think we even charged for what we did do.

We didn't have the needles we have now. I think the smallest we had was probably twenty-two gauge. When we'd see premature babies that needed fluids, we'd give them subcutaneous injections of normal saline between the scapula in the back and the sacrum in the back. I couldn't have found a vein, and couldn't have gotten a needle into one if I did, but you could give them about thirty or forty CCs that way. Our needles were reused, and there was usually a sharp hook on the tip of the point, so subcutaneous fluid was the only way we could do it.

The IV tubings were made out of rubber, and their outside diameter was about three-eighths to five-eighths inch in diameter. We would reuse them—wash them out with soap and water, then alcohol and ether, and then autoclave them. I would often take a quart bottle of dextrose solution, one of those bottles with a narrow neck on it, and put in a couple of salt tablets to make it into a normal saline solution.

Today we have good mammogram equipment at the clinic, and good X-ray equipment, but back when we moved up to Idaho Street we had one of those old rotating anode tube X-ray machines, with tank developing, and washing and fixing of the films by hand. I think that I'm probably the only doctor alive who failed to make the diagnosis of twin pregnancy on an abdominal X ray. I looked at the wet film, and put it away. Now we have acquired excellent X-ray equipment and have a good set-up at the clinic.

In thinking back, I realize how crude things were, how crude our laboratory was. It was as good as was available at that time, but it was still just counting chambers for white and red blood cell counts, and there was plenty of chance for error. But basically honest, good-quality medicine was practiced, and I learned a lot. One of the advantages for me of being with a group, even though it was a small group at that time, was the opportunity for curbstone consultations that didn't cost our patients a dime. It helped me give them better medicine, and it helped me to learn from more experienced doctors. That was a good feeling—I had backup all the time, and they were just as concerned about the patients as I was.

We never refused treatment for patients that didn't have any money. The county ran what we called the "poor farm" for elderly and destitute men, and we were responsible for supervising the medical care there. I think that the county paid us about $125, or maybe it was $100 a month for that work. The elderly women would be seen just like anybody else: they didn't have a nursing home, but the old Elko Hospital did have two wards, and one of them was reserved for elderly women. If we saw a patient in our office who was not able to pay, we just didn't put it on the books, and there was no discrimination as far as ability to pay was concerned. One of the advantages of being in a clinic group was that I didn't know who could pay and who couldn't, and I couldn't have cared less.

The ranchers often would pay us once a year, because they got paid once a year when they sold their cattle. During the Depression, before I got to Elko, a number of ranchers owed horrendous bills to the lumber company, the clothing stores, the power company, et cetera. Most of them were carried on credit, I think, without interest. When the Depression ended, those ranchers were really staunch supporters of the businesses that had carried them on credit.

There is an old story about two men who came into the barber shop, and when the first one's hair was cut, the barber asked him, "Do you want me to put some of that good-smelling tonic on your hair?"

He answered, "Oh, no! My wife would think I have been to a red-light house."

When the second one was done, the barber asked him the same thing, and the man replied, "You might just as well; my wife has never been in a red-light house!"

I guess there have been prostitutes in Elko since the middle 1800s, except for the period during World War II, when the Army Air Corps demanded that the houses be closed. I always thought it was interesting how they managed prostitution.

Basically they do it by licensing bars. There isn't any state law permitting prostitution, so it was regulated by the state liquor commission. There are, however, a number of county laws controlling just where the houses can be, and how they are operated, and that's the way it is done in most of the cow counties in Nevada.

The girls are supposed to be examined and have a smear to test for gonorrhea every week, and a blood test for syphilis every month. They are then given a certificate saying, "so-and-so was examined on this date and given a smear and blood test," or whatever. When you found a positive smear on one of the girls, you would just call the madam, and boy, was she anxious to get that girl out of her house! Our venereal disease rate has been very low, and I think it remains that way today. As a matter of fact, there would be more venereal disease among the men who would pick up a girl on the street than among those who patronize a red-light house.

Although I haven't any idea how much patronage the red-light houses get, I know that we have had very little rape in Elko and Elko County. These ranchers, miners, and sheepherders come in to get an outlet for their sexual urges, and if the red-light houses weren't around, they might be attacking women on the streets. Whether or not that's a good reason for legalized prostitution, I don't know, but it has become an accepted part of living in this part of the world.

There must be four or five red-light houses in the area, and when they have big conventions in town, I understand that the madams will call in extra gals, but the police restrict the girls' activities pretty carefully. They can't be on the street after five o'clock in the afternoon, and they can't patronize the downtown bars—the police are pretty strict about that, I think. I remember one madam, a good-looking lady probably in her fifties, said, "I've been in every illegal business you can think of—dope, rumrunning, gunrunning to Mexico, whatever was illegal—but in this town they have rules, and you expect to obey them." The licenses for the red-light houses are valuable, and the operators want to protect them.

Dr. Secor told me that one time during the war a lady who was a madam came to his office to ask his opinion about buying war bonds. He said, "Oh, it's a good thing." The next day she came in with a bag with $100,000 in cash to buy war bonds. That's a lot of cash, but I don't recall many robberies of the houses. One time a man came in to rob one of them, and he took the billfold or wallet from every patron in the place. The next day, one of the drug stores advertised, "Big sale on billfolds."

I haven't seen any of those girls as patients for a long, long time. I'll say this of the ones I have seen: none of the prostitutes or madams who came into our office ever acted any differently than anybody else. They were courteous, gentle people who behaved with excellent decorum. Except maybe by their dress, you couldn't have told that they were not just housewives. The madams behaved real respectably, too, and they never said bad words in the office or to the doctor. Yet some of them on the outside were just hard-bitten; they were real buzzards.

Shortly after the war, when penicillin first was available, one gal came in with pneumonia, sick as could be. She got well, and the madam treated her like she was her little child or something. The madam came to the office one time and showed me a picture of this gal, who had moved to California, married, and had twin babies. The madam here got her a double buggy for the kids, just as proud as any grandmother could be.

One time a gal called me in the middle of the night when the clinic was over on Idaho Street, and said, "Will you come down to the house and come in the back door?"

I said, "No, but I can meet you at the clinic. I'm not going in the back door of a whorehouse."

I went down to the office, and she said that she had been a prostitute in San Francisco, and had been on heroin. The habit had cost her seventy-five bucks a day for her drug. She wanted me to give her a shot of Demerol, a synthetic narcotic which is very addicting. I said, "I can't give you Demerol; I don't have any heroin, and I haven't seen any." I gave her a shot of Compazine or something like that and sent her on her way. That was that.

I haven't recognized that there is any greater use of drugs or alcohol amongst prostitutes compared to anybody else. Some experts claim that drug abusers resort to prostitution in order to get drugs, but I think that those are street prostitutes. I didn't recognize any mental differences in the prostitutes, either, except that they'd be pretty cynical, but their actions were perfectly normal when we'd see them in the office.

Bob Burns, the mortician here in Elko, ran the ambulance service around town as almost a gratis deal, and we made several runs together. One time we drove down to a mine in Crescent Valley. They had called and said, "A man is injured." A beam had fallen on him, and the industrial commission said they couldn't move an inch unless a doctor was there to OK it. "We'll meet you with a six-by-six truck to take you up there, and if you need medical supplies we can take an ambulance." The truck went through waist-high snow in the road for about a half mile and couldn't go any further, so we had to walk about four miles up a forty-five degree hill in soft snow. I was carrying a black bag, and it got heavier, heavier and heavier. When we got up there it was obvious the man had been killed instantly when the beam fell on him. We stripped off a piece of corrugated iron by hand, so that we could make a sort of toboggan, and then we lashed him it. The snow was so deep we had to *pull* it down the hill–it wouldn't slide down. We got back about seven o'clock in the morning . . . we had left about eight o'clock the night before. I wrote to the State Industrial Commission: "I don't know what you pay for this, but I won't do it again for a thousand dollars."

One time we went out to Ruby Valley to see a sick Indian. It was at night, and there are not many street lights out in Ruby Valley, and it was hard to find the place, but we finally stopped at a ranch house that had a generator. They had a light on in the yard, so we stopped to see if that was the place. "No, it's half a mile further down the valley." When we got there and walked into the house, I realized that I'd left my black bag at home. I was going in and didn't have a stethoscope or bandages or anything.

We entered this two-room house. The front room was maybe twelve-by-twelve feet and opened into a narrow, maybe twenty-foot long back room. There were sleeping bags on the floor with people in them, and there were two cots—one for the patient and one for an Indian lady. The man had white chalk painted on his left cheek and his arm and forearm and thighs.

I went over and had to look wise, you know. I said, "Well, I think we'd better take you to the hospital."

As we took him out on the gurney, the lady on the other cot said, "You take him to the hospital. I hex him; he die." By golly, he did die!

During that trip in from Ruby Valley we couldn't keep the ambulance warm because the radiator was losing water. We stopped at a running creek and found a leaky barrel to collect some more water to put into the radiator, but it ran dry almost immediately. Finally we got about seventeen miles east of Elko, to a place where they had a telephone, and called for help. They came out and took us in the rest of the way. We found out that the hose that brought the hot water from the engine to the heater in the back of the ambulance had dragged on the ground and worn a hole about an inch in diameter, so you could pour water into it all day long and it wouldn't do any good.

We used to see occasional cases of rattlesnake bite, but, I don't think I ever saw a fatal one. Our rattlesnakes here are not as large or as venomous as the Texas rattlesnakes. We have seen a few cases of tularemia in the past, but it is all hard for me to consider it nowadays in a differential diagnosis. There hasn't been a case of rabies in Elko County since 1903 that I know of, nor has there been a case of tetanus. You would think with horse country—where there are a lot of tetanus spores, and so on—that there would be, but I have never seen a case of it.

We did have a fair amount of trauma. In those days all of the haying was done with horse-drawn vehicles, and when they first started haying in the early summer, the horses had not been used all winter, so there were a lot of runaways. The ranch hands would get broken legs or sometimes a more serious injury. One time we got a fellow come in with a broken femur caused by a runaway, and the old rancher who employed him came in and asked Doc Roantree, "Can you date this tomorrow? If you will, I'll send in my Nevada Industrial Commission premium today."

Dr. Roantree said, "No, I can't do that."

The rancher was madder than seven hundred bucks. He hardly would ever talk to Dr. Roantree after that, because he had to assume personal financial responsibility for the ranch hand's injury.

We did, of course, make house calls in town, and every once in a while the railroad would call us to see a sick passenger on a train. We'd have to go down and try and make a quick diagnosis, and hope we had the stuff in our black bag to take care of them. I also made house calls out to ranches, and I think I used to charge a dollar a mile. Some of the ranchers would get as mad as they could be, because they thought that was just too much. We didn't charge them anything except the mileage, but some of those people couldn't afford to pay even that, you know. We would make house calls out to Carlin (eighteen miles), and even as far as Battle Mountain (sixty-seven miles).

We made many long, endless trips. Dr. Hadfield and one of the people from Bob Burns's ambulance service once went way up in the Rubys to see a sheepherder who was injured or sick in the hills. I think it took them eighteen hours to make the long trip, but that was what you had to do.

One time we got a call that a Greyhound bus was in an accident this side of Battle Mountain, in the valley where the highway makes a turn over the river. Dr. Jake Read and a nurse and I took off like cut cats and drove over there real fast. As we came into the valley by Battle Mountain, the sun was setting and it was just a beautiful red color. When we got down there, all the injured passengers had been taken into Battle Mountain. Nobody was seriously hurt, so we didn't even go on into Battle Mountain, because we knew that they didn't need us. It was a wild goose chase, but it was sure a pretty sunset!

The Western and Southern Pacific trains both run through Elko, and occasionally we'd be called to see passengers on one of the passenger trains. Doctor A. J. Hood was a life-long Republican; nearly as Republican as I am. Once we got a call from the railroad to come down and see a patient on the train. We were down at Dr. Hood's house at the time, and we didn't hear the phone ring, so they called Dr. Dale Hadfield, and he went down to the station to see the patient. The patient turned out to be Herbert Hoover and he was having a gallbladder attack.[†] Dale gave him a shot of morphine and sent him on his way, and some time later we got a beautiful letter from Herbert Hoover written from the Waldorf Towers in New York City. The letter was in appreciation for Dale's taking care of him. Dale made a mistake and told Dr. Hood what had happened, and Dr. Hood said, "I would have ridden the train all the way to Chicago to see Herbert Hoover!"

It was a big job for people living on distant, outlying ranches to make the trip into town, so we used to make a fair number of trips out to the ranches in the 1950s and early 1960s.

[†] Herbert Clark Hoover (Republican) was President of the United States from 1929 to 1933.

We made several trips by bush-pilot airplane to pick up people. That always intrigued me. The first, I think, was in April of 1946, when I got a call from way up on the Bruneau River. You could get in there by road from Idaho, but it took about three days to go by car or horse from Elko, so I flew up. They said they'd light a big bonfire so we could tell what field to land in, but when we got up there I couldn't see any. The pilot says, "There it is." There was about as much smoke as from a cigarette. The pilot landed the plane in the field, and the rancher had a horse there, so I got on the horse and carried my black bag down the winding canyon. When I got down there, they said their boy was home from the military, and he had had pneumonia. I had brought along a shot of penicillin and some penicillin pills, and I listened to his chest and thought he still had pneumonia, so I gave him a penicillin shot and left the penicillin pills.

They wrote me out a check, and I got on the horse and went back up to the field. The pilot said, "This is a short field and pretty high altitude, and we are going to have to jump the plane to get it off of the ground." We dragged the airplane by hand over to the fence line, and he gunned the motor, and we'd go a little bit and jump a little bit and down again to gather speed. Got over the end of the field, and he turned it on its wing, and we had to go about three hundred and sixty degrees. I could have reached over and picked up some willows on the way.

When we got back to town, I went to the drug store and paid for the penicillin I had gotten. It cost me eighteen dollars for the penicillin and I had charged the family twenty-five dollars, so it wasn't a very profitable day; but it was fun.

In the early 1950s we had one plane trip during the summer time—during haying season—up to the Tuscarora area, where a man had fallen off a haystack. They said they'd have a white sheet out to tell us where to land. When the pilot got up there and looked for the field, he found it OK, but it was at the mouth of a canyon. He said, "I could never get out of there," so we landed in another field, and they came over to get us. (The plane stopped about two or three feet in front of a foot-deep ditch, just wham!)

The man had a broken back, so we couldn't take him back in the airplane. We brought him in on a pick-up rig, lying on a mattress in the back of the truck. We arched his back in order to prevent any further damage, but he was paralyzed, and we sent him down to San Francisco by train. Before he left we put him on a Stryker fracture frame. (It took a couple of years before the hospital in San Francisco sent the Stryker frame back to our hospital.) They couldn't put him in a passenger car, so they had to put him in the mail car. He later died of the broken back, because the spinal cord was severed.

Another time I got a call from up north, from a lady in the family of Jimmy Stewart, the motion picture star. She said, "One of my twin daughters has been sick for about three days. Can you come up and see her?"

I said, "Sure."

"She is up at the Wine Cup Ranch north of Wells. You charter a plane and come up here, and we'll meet you." So we landed at a little strip there, and the cloud of dust from the propeller was just horrendous. She took me to the house where the girl was, and after I examined her I thought she had appendicitis, possibly perforated. I said, "Well, I will take the airplane, and you drive back with the girl and meet us in Elko." She drove so fast that the car almost beat the plane back. We got back to the hospital, and I asked Hugh Collett see her. The family knew a famous surgeon in Chicago, and they weren't really very sure if they should trust their daughter to a bunch of country doctors, so they asked if we would call and talk to the surgeon in Chicago.

Hugh told me, "You talk to the doctor."

The Chicago surgeon asked, "What was the erythrocyte count?"

"We didn't do an erythrocyte count, but white count was 22,000, with a shift to the left. The surgeon here is a board-certified surgeon."

"OK, let me talk to him about it."

He talked to Hugh, and he told him, "Go ahead."

She got along OK, but she worried the daylights out of us. The equipment we had was good state-of-the-art equipment for those times, but now it would look pretty antiquated.

Another earlier patient from up there was a pregnant patient. I think that the husband's first wife had died in childbirth, and the husband would call me once or twice a week to check on how everything was progressing. Everything was fine, and she delivered a normal, healthy baby after a normal pregnancy. We didn't know what to charge her. She was wealthy, and sometimes I think wealthy people feel bad if you undercharge them, so I talked to Hugh Collett about it, and we charged them, I think, six hundred dollars. A friend in Los Angeles later told me, "You dope! Down here it would have been five thousand dollars!" But she got along OK, and we've been friends ever since.

I had to fly out to see one of Bing Crosby's boys at his Tuscarora ranch one time. I thought that we should wait and see how he was doing, but the pilot said, "Hey, we've got to get back, Doc! I don't want to wait until it gets dark. I don't want to fly uncharted airways at night." We got back OK, and the boy did fine.

Bing Crosby was always a gracious, wonderful person, a friend to me, and he was a fun person to be around. When he was at his ranch, he worked just like the buckaroos. He was unassuming, and one of the things he liked best about Elko was that people didn't fawn over him like a movie actor. He was just accepted as another buckaroo, another friend, just like the rest.

John and Doris Eckert were good friends of mine. John worked for Bing managing his ranch, and Doris helped John with the ranch and helped raise the Crosby boys. She flew in the

Powder Puff Derby for several years.[†] John and Doris are both dead now.

Flying down to Beowawe was always a little hairy, I guess, but I was never real apprehensive because the pilots I flew with were good bush pilots. Two of the people that I flew with have since died, one in an airplane crackup, and the other one of natural causes.

One time when we flew out to Ruby Valley our plane was equipped with skis, because there was snow on the ground. I wanted the patient to come in with us, because she was suffering from what I thought was a phlebitis. She needed hospitalization, but the snow plow hadn't come through yet, and the road was impassable. We got into the plane, I got in the back seat, and the pilot started the engine and made several tries at taking off. Then the pilot said, "Doctor, you're going to have to get out. You are too heavy, and I can't get off of the ground." So I climbed out and went back to the house. After the snow plow came through, the rancher drove me to Wells, and I caught a bus from Wells to Elko. These were all good people. You became friends with these people, because they knew that you would put yourself out to accommodate them.

One time I saw a little girl about four or five years old. We were still having polio cases, and I had seen her a few days before for a cold or something, and they called me over to see her again. Gosh, I thought she had polio, so we got Burns and Newt Crumley to fly us into Salt Lake City with the little girl. We were giving her oxygen, but we ran out of it when we were still ten miles this side of Salt Lake. So we made an emergency call for oxygen before we got there. They met us with the ambulance and took her right to the hospital. Come to find out, she didn't have polio at all: she had overdosed on a cough syrup

---

[†] A cross-country air race for women pilots, sponsored by the organization of woman pilots, the 99s.

that had codeine in it, and she just acted like she had polio. (There hasn't been a case of acute poliomyelitis in Elko since 1955. I always worry that it is not going to be in my index of suspicion when I see a patient that might have polio. We've seen a few cases of Guillain-Barré, which scares the living daylights out of me, and I'm never sure if I know how to make the diagnosis. I guess it's as much by the history as it is anything by any thing else.)

We stayed overnight at a hotel in Salt Lake City. Newt Crumley, of course, was well known all over. He said, "Well, we ought to have a Scotch and soda." He called down and asked for Scotch and soda. Utah is a dry state, but Newt talked to the manager of the hotel, and he got a bottle of Scotch for him right away.

People like Newt and other friends really were solid citizens. I keep thinking how we were blessed. Elko was such a wonderful place to be and to live, and I enjoyed it very much. (They named the airport in Elko after Jess Harris, who was Sheriff of Elko County for many years. His dad was the sheriff before him, and Neil Harris was elected sheriff last fall; I think he's a relative, but not Jess's son. Jess Harris was lackadaisical–when you met him on the street he would say, "¿Cómo está?")

The first time I had to appear as a witness in the Elko District Court, Orville Wilson, a local attorney, had been appointed by the court to defend a Basque sheepherder who was charged with killing two men–I think he had shot them right out in the open, shooting them intentionally. Orville asked me to see the defendant as a physician. I was allowed about fifteen minutes to visit with him, but he spoke no English and I spoke no Basque, so the communication wasn't very good.

When the case came to trial, the district attorney asked me if I was a psychiatrist. "No," I told him, "I worked at a nervous and mental hospital for a couple of years, but I am not a psychiatrist."

"What do you think of him?"

"Well," I answered, "I think the defendant ought to have a real psychiatric consultation."

The judge said, "Elko County can't afford that."

He was judged guilty, and they sent him down to the gas house at the Nevada state prison. When they dumped the pellet of cyanide into acid, he held his breath, and you'd swear he wouldn't take another one. It took five minutes before he took another breath and died.

It wasn't that we were insensitive, but in those days before we had airplane travel, we couldn't always transfer patients to Salt Lake City, Reno, San Francisco, or even as far as Denver . . . wherever they wished to go. I think the people of this community, many of them, do not realize what expert medical and surgical care they got from Tom Hood and Hugh Collett in general surgery, orthopedics, and OB-GYN surgery.

Dr. A. J. Hood, Tom's dad, was instrumental in getting the legislature to enact legislation enabling Elko County to build Elko County General Hospital. I think that passed in 1919, and the hospital then opened in 1921. It was built sort of on the plan of St. Francis Hospital in San Francisco, which already was a little bit out of date architecturally, but at least it served the purpose. In 1937 they added a surgery wing and some rooms for nurses' quarters, and we had a small isolation building which we called the Pest House behind the hospital for contagious diseases like scarlet fever, measles, and polio. Of course, that was the vogue at that time, but is done no more at all. The hospital became accredited by the Joint Commission during Dr. Roantree's lifetime. We had, perhaps, thirty-five beds, including two four-bed wards. There was one creaky elevator, but it worked.

When I came to Elko, the nurses were paid ninety dollars a month for a seventy-two hour week, and they got their board and room. They got nurses through the tremendous efforts of Marie Herbester, who was the superintendent of nurses and chief nurse when I came here. She was also the hospital administrator. She was the only one who could fix the elevator; she was the only one who could fix the furnace; she'd mow the lawn in her spare time. We had good nurses. Most of them were graduates from three-year nursing schools, which were common in those days.

It wasn't until 1960, probably, that we got nurse anesthetists who were well trained, and now we've got excellent nurse anesthetists, but we don't have any M.D. anesthesiologists. One man called me a few years ago, an M.D. anesthesiologist, wondering what the job opportunities would be here for him. "Well," I said, "we don't have any M.D. anesthesiologists; we have nurse anesthetists. We get twenty-four-hour-a-day coverage, and they are always available. They can get here in five minutes, anytime. I wouldn't want to lose that kind of service in order to get an M.D. anesthesiologist." That is still the case. Obviously they are not M.D.'s, but, boy, they are well trained. They care about their patients, and I think they do an excellent job.

That first expansion to the Elko County Hospital was in 1937, and then about 1957 they built a whole new wing, which included surgery, X ray, lab and outpatient care. Later they tore down the old building and rebuilt the new section. They've done some interior remodeling since then, and added a mobile trailer home for administrative offices. We're due to have a new X-ray machine, radioactive isotope scanner, and a CAT (computerized axial tomography) scanner. They also remodeled the obstetrics wing in 1957, and did a good job.[†]

I think that the population of Elko has quadrupled in the last ten years, but the hospital facilities still seem to be adequate. You've got to remember that nowadays patients have shorter

---

[†] The obstetrical wing of Elko General Hospital, built in 1957, is named the Leslie A. Moren wing.

hospital stays. You know, the patient goes home two days after a gallbladder operation or whatever, and sometimes the same day after they have a baby. They have a hospital pharmacy and excellent clinical laboratory facilities, with well-qualified technologists.

I don't know what the financial arrangements are now, but everybody at the clinic divided the pot equally until about ten or fifteen years ago. Then we had a bad experience with an orthopedist. We always would sign a contract for a six-months trial period, to see if the doctor liked us and if we liked the doctor. We found out, when this orthopedist had been here about three months, that he was already printing up cards saying he was going to open up his own office in Elko, and we learned that he was postponing orthopedic surgery until then.

We had a restrictive covenant in the contract, that if a doctor left the clinic he couldn't practice in competition with the clinic within a certain distance for two years. After he left the clinic, we sued this man and got a judgment against him. A local judge granted our injunction. Then the orthopedist got a preliminary injunction against us, and got a hearing before the state supreme court. It was the first time they had heard a case on a preliminary injunction. They ruled against us, and the judge who heard us at the trial said, "Well, obviously, I can't please both sides." It took about six months before he gave us a verdict. In the meantime the first judgment was $130,000, with $30,000 for the attorney's fees. We were able to get that $30,000 knocked off, but the court gave a judgment to the doctor for $100,000 plus interest, which was $12,000 over the six months.

After that experience, the group decided that we could not attract a highly-trained specialist with an even division of the income, so the contract was changed to basically a minimum salary, but with additional income based on productivity. I think that this has taken a little bit of the one-for-all, all-for-one spirit away from the group. The camaraderie is a little bit different, and we've had doctors come and go since then, partly because of the economics, I think.

Although other doctors here in Elko have served on the Elko General Hospital board of trustees, those of us in the Elko Clinic never have. We felt that it might be looked on as a conflict of interest, since some of the clinic members, such as the radiologist and pathologist, are also employed by the hospital. Members of the clinic do, of course, serve their turns as officers on the hospital's medical staff, because everyone has to be involved in those jobs.

When Mike O'Callaghan was elected governor of Nevada in 1970, one of his platforms was getting health care to rural areas. At that time the hospital was sponsoring a nurse practitioner in Wells, and the governor wanted the doctors to have satellite offices in all the little towns that couldn't support a doctor on their own. We considered it, and we were going to hire nurse practitioners, but we consulted with our malpractice insurance company, and they said, "Boy, if you do that, we'll drop you like a hot potato." Governor O'Callaghan became very angry at the clinic, because we refused to open satellite clinics, and he wouldn't even listen to our explanation for it. We would have tried it, if the hospital had sponsored it, for we could have acted as consultants, but if the clinic sponsored it, then we had to bear the brunt of the liability, and our insurance company said, "No way."

Today the clinic, which has been renamed the Elko Regional Medical Center, does operate satellite medical offices in Battle Mountain and Spring Creek for the convenience of the people who live in those areas. The populations of these communities have boomed in the past few years after the big increase in mining activity in Elko County. The doctors from the clinic would rotate down to Battle Mountain and spend a period of time there. They do have a doctor, an M.D., down in Battle Mountain now; they used to have an osteopathic physician, Dr.

Bannister. I have only met the new doctor once, so I don't know him very well, and I haven't even been inside the clinic at Spring Creek yet. It's been in operation only a couple of months or so. We had to open the satellite clinic at Spring Creek because the population out there has sky-rocketed to over eight thousand people.

6

SOME MEMORABLE CASES

THE LIFE OF A general practitioner is hectic, but in some ways it can be routine. I delivered lots of babies, and I treated countless patients for colds, flu, pneumonia, measles, chicken pox, broken bones, and all the other ailments that are so common among people everywhere. Every now and then, however, I would get a case that was unforgettable:

I had scrubbed on surgical cases of all kinds, but the first time you are the chief surgeon and it is up to you . . . God, it's a different ball game! The first time I had to do an appendix alone, Dr. Roantree was gone. He had left on a Sunday for a medical meeting, and on Monday I was called to the Elko Auto Court (where the clinic building now stands) to see a sick lady. I was sure she had acute appendicitis. Not being a surgeon, but having assisted on a lot of appendectomies, I knew what I was supposed to do, so I operated on her. (I *had* to operate on the patient, for in those days transportation wasn't a cup of tea, and moving her to another hospital was out of the question.) She got along fine.

Two days later Dr. Roantree was still gone, and I had another acute appendicitis. In those days you were kept in the hospital a week or more after an appendectomy, you know. They both got along OK, but when we took out the second one's stitches, the wound just dehisced–the skin edges split apart. He didn't have ileus (bowel distention), and the belly wall had healed up all right, but the skin had not. I took out the stitches and the skin edges just fell apart like there was no approximation at all. No skin healing . . . that has haunted me ever since. Anyway, we sewed him up again and he healed fine. Some years later I had to take out his brother's appendix, and the same thing happened to him. I thought in retrospect, "I wonder if those boys were vitamin-C deficient?"

It may have been that same weekend that a deer hunter from California came in with prostatic obstruction of the urethra. He couldn't void. His bladder was up to his umbilicus, and I couldn't get into it with a catheter or with a Foley, a sound, a filiform, or anything . . . and I wasn't smart enough just to put a big long needle through the belly wall to decompress his bladder. Finally, I did a suprapubic cystotomy, put in a mushroom catheter, and sewed it in there. He got along fine. He wrote to me after he got back to California and gave me hell. He asked, "Why did you operate on me?" Well, you have to do what you think is best.

The first time I had to do a cesarean section alone was after the war. George Collett, Hugh's dad, had left on the morning plane to go to Chicago for an American College of Surgeons meeting; Tom Hood left on the evening plane. A gal came in at term with placenta previa, and I had to do a section. It was either me or God, and they couldn't find God's scalpel, so I got a crew together. Well, the night floor nurse didn't have the right pair of glasses, and the scrub nurse came in, and she had had two or three Scotches, so she wasn't worth too much . . . . Dr. Secor gave the patient drip ether anesthesia, and things went OK, and we got a good baby. I tied the patient's tubes, because it was the lady's fourth baby. I never told her that she was the first one I had ever done a C-section on alone, and I never admitted how nervous I was.

I once helped Tom Hood and Hugh Collett operate on a man with a ruptured abdominal aneurysm. We had the whole crew there working on him, but in spite of our best efforts the man died. Another late afternoon or night there were four of us at the hospital working on a man who had been thrown out of a jeep and ground against a curbstone. He was actually quartered when he got into the hospital–there were four of us doctors working. I think we gave him thirty units of blood transfusion, and we were clamping off bleeders, doing this, that and the other thing, but we just had to watch him die.

One weekend a big, hefty Indian from Owyhee came in with a red-hot gallbladder. He had to have something done, so I did a cholecystotomy and put in a mushroom catheter, but I didn't try to take out the stone. He survived. (Some years later, after everything calmed down, Tom Hood and Hugh Collett did a cholecystectomy on him.) At the time I felt scared and apprehensive . . . . I had to do a lot of things that I really didn't feel comfortable doing, but I think what it boils down to is that the people who taught me, taught me well.

A lady who was a member of the Jehovah's Witness organization was hurt in a car wreck. She came in with multiple severe injuries, and we felt she needed blood transfusions, but both she and her husband absolutely refused permission for us to transfuse her, and we just had to watch her die. The last hemoglobin reading we got on her was one gram, which is about 7 percent of the normal level.

The Rh factor wasn't discovered until 1940, and good typing serum wasn't available until about 1946. (The early testing serum was not too reliable.) We would always cross-match blood, and if we got Rouleaux formation we would know that we couldn't use that blood, although we didn't know why. We didn't know anything about the Rh factor, and I think that perhaps I contributed to one lady's death because of it. I gave her a transfusion of blood that had typed and cross-matched OK, but she developed a severe jaundice and died, I think probably from a reaction to Rh incompatible blood.

We haven't had very many cases of erythroblastosis fetalis, or the so-called blue babies. One time a doctor in town asked me to see a baby that was three days old and very jaundiced, apparently due to Rh incompatibility. Tom Hood and I spent the whole afternoon doing an exchange transfusion. That was tough treatment on a newborn, and we kept an anesthetist handy in case of a bad reaction. The baby did get along OK, but I'm sure he had some kernicterus.[†] He has been a little bit retarded, but not drastically. After Rhogam testing became available as a routine, we were careful about that; that was the one thing that we tried to make sure of.

We've had other babies born with fetal-maternal blood type incompatibility (Big D-little e; that sort of thing), but usually we were able to recognize that quickly enough. When airplane transportation became available, we'd transport them into Salt Lake City, usually to the Primary Children's Hospital, where they had special laboratories and a good blood supply available. They could cross-match for all the less common blood factors, like c, d, e, Kell, and those less common ones. That always was, and it still remains, pretty much a mystery to me–knowing which patients needed the testing. Of course, if you got a history from them about difficulties with previous pregnancies, then a doctor would know when to test.

We had trouble with one baby with c-e incompatibility. When the mother had her next child, we arranged in advance to get blood of the right type, and we successfully transfused that

---

[†] Desposition of bile pigment into the nuclei of brain cells of the newborn due to jaundice, which may result in mental retardation.

baby. One of those babies we sent in to Primary Children's. They have always been very gracious to us, and, I think, most patients appreciated that. After rural transportation became pretty good you could send patients to Reno, Salt Lake City, or most any place in relatively short order. It's not always inexpensive, but at least you're doing the best thing you can for the patient.

One time I saw a little Indian child, about four or five years old, who came in and had an obvious meningococcal meningitis with a rash and a stiff neck. I saw her at the office and took her right over to the hospital, but she was dead within thirty minutes. Two or three days later, while I was attending a meeting somewhere, Jake saw a sister of that child, and *she* came in and died within about four hours. We don't see too many cases of meningococcal meningitis, thank goodness! The treatment now is fairly successful if you get it started early enough, but when we went to medical school, meningitis was always a devastating, almost 100 percent fatal disease.

Tuberculosis is very rare now, but it used to be pretty common up at the Indian reservation in Owyhee. Here within the last six months one of the doctors in the clinic picked up a tuberculous kidney, which is pretty doggoned rare. There was also a TB of the scrotum here not too long ago, a scrotum that had a draining sinus and didn't seem to respond to the usual treatment, and we found some acid-fast organisms in the drainage. That's not very common.

Shortly after the war, I got a call to see a lady about six o'clock one morning. She had been on a three-day drunk somewhere up in Idaho, and when she came back to Elko she said she had a hell of a toothache. Actually, what she had was Ludwig's angina. Boy, I took her right up to the hospital in my own car, gave her a huge dose of penicillin, 100,000 units, and called Dr. Roantree and Dr. Secor down to see her in consultation. About six o'clock that night she convulsed and died.

A. J. Hood was an excellent diagnostician. One time I saw a man who had eosinophilia, and had a sort of bronzed belt around the skin of his back. Dr. Hood said, "Maybe he's got carcinoma of the pancreas." He was just as right as rain. He and Dr. Secor probably were the first ones to make the connection between sick rabbits and tularemia, but they never recorded it. Had they done so, it might have been called "Elkoremia". He also diagnosed a couple of cases of typhoid–one case of typhoid fever, and one a typhoid carrier.

We did have typhoid and diphtheria cases and Rocky Mountain spotted fever, Colorado tick fever, and other diseases that are seen very seldom now. Chloromycetin was the first drug that came along that would cure Rocky Mountain spotted fever, which had a mortality rate of 15 percent. (I think one time in Montana the mortality was about 85 percent.) After it became available Dr. Secor said, "Gosh, I hope we have a case of Rocky Mountain spotted fever." We got two cases at the same time. Before then patients with Rocky Mountain spotted fever were in the hospital four to six weeks, and they couldn't work all summer because they were just knocked out, but both of these men were in the hospital just five days, went home, and went back to work in two weeks.

One of them who lived in Montello came in after he'd been in the hospital. "Gee, Doc," he said, "that medicine that you gave me cost me fifty bucks."

I explained, "If every fifty bucks you spent saved you that much money, you'd be lucky."

"OK, I'll quit bitchin'," he said. Now, some of these antibiotics are $100 a shot.

One time a patient came in who had been taking the drug lithium for a manic depressive psychosis. Her husband had tripled her dose, and she came in with a big overdose. For three days she didn't even move an eyelid–she breathed once in a while, and that was it. We didn't know how in the dickens to treat it, so we gave her IVs, trying to wash out the overdose.

A lady who had had rheumatic fever, a longtime friend, came to work for me in my private office before we started the clinic. She was a laboratory technician, one of the first well-trained lab technicians in town. She had rheumatic heart disease. She developed an infection, and I thought a septicemia. I gave her a million units of penicillin every twelve hours (or maybe every day; whatever it was), and she wasn't getting any better. She had a rheumatic heart valve, and I was afraid she would develop a bacterial endocarditis. We sent her down to San Francisco, and the first thing they did was increase her dosage to twenty million units of penicillin in a constant drip. She did well. She later died of an acute myocardial infarction, but she didn't develop subacute bacterial endocarditis.

We've seen a few cases of disseminated lupus, which is such a disheartening disease: it makes you feel so inadequate Because you are not able to offer any real treatment. We had one young lady die of disseminated lupus—we were able to make the diagnosis, and had it confirmed by a specialist elsewhere, and we just had to watch her go down the tube and die. With another case of lupus, the patient was on steroids, and she didn't tell us. She came into the hospital with a paroxysmal auricular tachycardia, and we admitted her, and she died a short time later. She had a distended stomach, and I think she inhaled gastric contents.

We've treated bad burns of various kinds—some electrical burns, and some fire burns from kerosene and gasoline. In the early days, in the 1940s and 1950s, we almost always ended up with bad scarring, but over the years we've vastly changed their treatment, with the introduction of antibiotic ointments, creams, jellies, et cetera. Sulfa drugs were available early on, of course, but penicillin didn't become generally available until about 1946. We used what we considered to be huge doses—10,000 units every three hours around the clock. Changing dressings used to be a horrible ordeal when there were large burned areas. Of course, all we had was ether anesthesia, and we hated to put a patient who was sick with severe burns under general anesthesia just to change dressings every day.

I remember one man who was a helicopter pilot from one of the big ranches up north. He took off and got a hundred or so feet into the air when something happened to the helicopter, and it crashed and burned. He had burns over his entire body except for where his shoes had covered his feet and ankles. We could hardly get a needle through his burned skin, for it was just like leather. We called the Army burn center down in Texas, as well as the ones in Orange County and San Francisco, but they couldn't help us, and he died after about two days. We felt bad, but I don't think he would have survived even if we could have gotten him to one of the burn centers.

A young man who had been shot in the head came in. The bullet had entered in his forehead, and the exit wound was in the occiput. The bullet hadn't penetrated the skull at all; it had gone up under the scalp and around and out. That sure surprised the daylights out of all of us.

I was helping Tom Hood one day with a man that came in after a car wreck. He had either a subdural or epidural hematoma in his head (I can't remember which now) but he came in walking perfectly, and was quite rational . . . when all of a sudden he became unconscious. Under local anesthesia, I helped Tom open a flap in his skull and suck out the blood clot. Pretty soon he was waking up a little bit and getting sort of rambunctious. I had to leave about then to go deliver a baby, but after the delivery I came back to help Tom some more. About then the nurse came in and said, "Your OB is bleeding," so I had to go back to see her. By the time I finally got back, the man got along OK. Tom and I used to get Christmas cards from him every year for twenty or so years.

7

A PHYSICIAN'S LIFE IN ELKO

WHEN I ARRIVED IN Elko in 1938 there was a big group of young people about my age who were compatible and friendly. We had parties in our homes, or we'd go down to the Commercial Hotel when they had the floor shows. It would cost you five bucks for you and your date, so we couldn't really afford more than about four of them a year. The Commercial Hotel had a lot of big-name entertainers, and that was always a social event. The Elks Lodge would put on a big dance once a year, and that was also a big social event. Sometimes people would rent the lodge and have big parties, but most frequently there were parties at friends' homes. Really intimate, close friendships developed, for it was a group of people that made you feel real comfortable to be around.

When we started our clinic, Dr. George Collett said that we clinic members should not limit our social lives to the other partners and the other doctors, because then you get inborn errors of metabolism, so to speak. It wasn't that the doctors didn't enjoy one another's company, but we tried not to confine our social activities just to other physicians, which probably was wise. It wasn't too objective a rule, but nobody ever challenged it. We found mutual friendships that have lasted all these years.

One of the things that impressed me when I first came to Elko was the Commercial Hotel.[†] It had a big lobby with big, leatherette-covered stuffed chairs, and a rancher'd be sitting next to a cattle buyer like you and I are talking now. And the rancher'd say, "Well, I've got about so many cattle I think that weigh about so much."

And the cattle buyer would say, "Well, I'll pick them up on October 15, and pay you so much a pound." They never even shook hands; they didn't sign any papers; and they didn't have any lawyers. Each of them knew the other man would keep his end of the bargain, unless he had a broken neck. A big trust. Back then people generally trusted others until they found some reason not to trust them.

The owner of the Commercial Hotel, Newt Crumley, attended one of the early Army flying schools, Kelly Field, down in Texas. When he graduated in about 1937, he was sent to Selferidge Field in Michigan. His outfit there had to do so many hours of stunt flying, so many hours of nighttime flying, and so much cross-country daytime flying. He had to bail out in a parachute over Pennsylvania when the Army was flying the mail one time, and he wasn't hurt from the landing, except that the car that picked him up to take him into town was in an accident and he got hurt some. About ten years later I took a hunk of glass out of his thigh; it had been there all that time. He had to bail out again while he was flying in California, I think, during the war. (Twice he got whatever the recognition is that you get if you survive a parachute jump out of an Army plane.)

[†] The Commercial Hotel was owned by Newton H. Crumley, Sr., and his son Newton H. Crumley, Jr., who was an aviator. Newt Crumley, Jr., named his son Newton H. Crumley III.

Newt became a colonel in the air force, and the commandant of Minter Field, a training field in California, I think. He would never let them cashier a potential pilot, or throw him out, unless he personally took him up in a plane and observed his flying capabilities. The men under him either loved him or hated him. He was a little bit spit and polish, but he damned well knew airplanes, and he was a good flyer.

When he came back from the air force, Newt took over as owner and manager of the Commercial hotel. Before the war–just to show you what kind of business man he was–he bought a whole railroad car load of Ten High Whiskey, which filled up the whole basement storage space of the Commercial Hotel. Everybody told him he was crazy. Well, it wasn't very long before the war came along and you couldn't buy whiskey. He could sell it at twenty-five cents a shot and make money on it.

Newt was a mover. The first floor shows in Nevada were in the Commercial Hotel, and when Newt was flying me down to Los Angeles one time to see a friend of his, I said, "You can't be making any money on those floor shows." They were a week long you know, with famous people like Ted Fiorito and Sophie Tucker and other famous names. I said, "You can't make any money on them," because he had no minimum, no cover charge or anything. "Oh, no," he says. "If I break even, I'm luckier than a lot, but if I can advertise Elko, I'll get my share of the dollars that roll in."

They had Paul Whiteman and his band and Ted Fiorito . . . and who was the guy that played the clarinet? His theme song was "Me and My Shadow". They had Sophie Tucker and Eddie Peabody. There were big dance bands that would come there and play, with never any cover charge, and no minimum, and that was a wholesome, good thing for Elko. There have not really been too many entrepreneurs that had that idea: it seems like most of them have the attitude that you have to make a profit on every part of the operation, you know. Newt could charge part of the costs as a tax write-off, but it was a smart move on his part–Elko became known among the show people of that time. Elko people can be pretty discriminating audiences, and performers used to tell me when I'd visit with them that if they could make it in Elko, they could make it any place in the world, because Elko was a tough audience. You didn't get by with just a second-rate show.

Newt had a policy that every entertainment outfit he hired had to give a free concert at the high school auditorium, because the school kids couldn't come down to the bar where liquor was served. So he had the groups go up to the high school auditorium . . . . Well, they didn't mind. Newt would never permit any bad language, or language that was suggestive, and all of the entertainers knew it. Sophie Tucker was probably the only one that got by with her line of talk.

One time a group came in to open on Saturday night at nine o'clock, and they were supposed to give a second floor show at eleven o'clock. During the first floor show there was a chorus line of girls, and Newt thought it was a little too vulgar, so he told them "You are done here, and you are not going to give a second performance here tonight." So he called . . . I believe Sam Ruby was the booking agent in San Francisco, and Newt said, "Sam, these girls are out; we'll need a new group here by tomorrow night."

"God, it's Saturday night, I can't do it that soon."

Newt said, "That's our contract," and there was a new group Sunday night. Newt Crumley established a high level of performance and consideration for morals. Not that everybody was real moral or moralistic, mind you, but there was certainly nothing that would contribute to moral delinquency.

One time Newt called and said, "I've got an Army plane and I've got to put some flying hours in. Where would you like to go for dinner?"

I said, "What do you mean?"

He said, "Oh, Denver, San Francisco, or Las Vegas; let's go to Las Vegas." We flew down to Las Vegas, and it was hotter than the hinges of Hades. There were only a few places that you could eat; one was the Sal Sagev, which is Las Vegas spelled backwards. Most of the eating places were right by the Union Pacific depot. We came back on a night flight from Las Vegas to Salt Lake, and then Salt Lake to Elko, because they had radio signal beacons. That was the first time I had ever been in an airplane at night, and it was a beautiful sight for me, and very thrilling,

Newt took another man and me up one time in a Stearman airplane. It used about as many quarts of oil as it did gallons of gasoline, I think. He flew us to hunt Hungarian partridges up around Boise, Idaho. The other fellow had a dog named Bessie, a bird dog. We were out hunting, and it was hot and dusty, and Newt and I were up on the banks of a dry creek bed, and the other man was down there in the bottom of the creek bed with his dog, when a couple of birds flew up. Bang! Bang! He shot them both. Newt said, "Don't do that! Those birds are pheasants and they're out of season."

The guy said, "Oh, hell; this dog wouldn't raise a bird out of season." He was determined to keep them, but we didn't dare keep them inside the car, because they were illegal; so we took off a hub cap and put the two birds inside the it, so that if we were stopped by a game warden, he wouldn't find them. We were just scared to death the whole time.

Newt was a good friend of Bing Crosby, and he went on trips with Bing, hunting in Idaho and so on. He did a lot of traveling. He sponsored a Skeet Club, and he'd take them first class any place they wanted to go to skeet meets.

His father was still alive when Newt built his home, so on the first floor Newt had them build a special room and bathroom for his dad. His home was one of the nicest homes in Elko. In the air force he had learned how to play squash, and he was a good squash player, so when he built his home, he built a squash court in it. After his home was completed he found out that the squash court was one foot shorter than regulation, so he knocked out the whole wall and rebuilt the darn thing! We'd come in the back door and play squash, and never even enter the house itself.

Newt was a staunch Republican who became state senator from Elko County, and he was also on the board of regents at the university.[†] He was late for one board of regents meeting because he and his family were on a sailboat down to the Caribbean, and there was a storm, and he got sloshed over and had to take a plane to get home; but he never missed a meeting.

Newt had the ability to turn on a smile as quickly as anybody I've ever known. When he was running for state senator, he was running against a Democrat, Snowy Monroe, who was a good friend of mine; I thought the world of him. I had a cabin out in Lamoille, and Newt asked me if I would go with him to campaign out there. I said sure, but when we went out he knew more of the folks there than I did, really.

One time Newt took Orv Wilson (an Elko attorney) and me down to San Francisco to play squash at the Olympic Club. My wife and Orv's wife went along, but Newt's wife couldn't go because of illness. When we got into the Palace Hotel in San Francisco, Newt called down and asked for a ringside table for the five of us (one of the Noble boys' orchestra was playing there), but they said the tables were all taken. He said, "I'm Newt Crumley from the Commercial Hotel in Elko, and I want a table." By God, we got it too! That was the first time in my life I ever had Cherries Jubilee. Newt treated us great. Orv and I could no more afford that trip than the man in the moon, but Newt picked up the tab for the whole thing—he wouldn't even consider letting us pay. I would guess that in that era, Newt probably spent more loot than anybody else I ever knew. It really wasn't ostentation; it was just the way he was.

[†] Crumley served two terms in the Nevada State Senate, 1955-1957 and 1957-1959. He also served three terms as a University of Nevada regent: 1950-1954; 1958-1960; and 1960-1964.

One of his friends and I were seat mates on a plane together after Newt's death, and he told me, "Newt would be a millionaire one day, and a million dollars in debt the next." That could be. He moved to Reno and bought the Holiday Hotel, which didn't have gambling then–just the Riverside and Mapes did. Some of my friends from Reno said, "What kind of guy is this Crumley from Elko?"

I said, "Well, I'll tell you this: the Mapes and the Riverside are going to realize that they've got competition once he opens up." And they did. Newt had really good taste, sometimes to the point that it might be unnecessarily costly, but everything that he did was done with flourish and aplomb, and he had a busy business.

I think it was 1962 when Newt and a fellow who was president of the First National Bank in Nevada, Eddie Questa, were down in Palm Springs at some meeting. They were advised not to fly back to Elko that Saturday night, because the weather was bad. Well, Newt figured he was a good pilot, and that he could handle it. The last they heard from him, he was over Tonopah and requested permission to climb to seventeen thousand feet because the airplane was icing up. That was the last they heard. Later they went out and found the wreckage of the plane in Smoky Valley near Tonopah, not very far from where Newt was born. They must have been going seven hundred miles per hour when they hit the ground, and they were really clobbered. Newt was fifty years old when he was killed, but he lived as many years in those fifty as most of us could live if we lived to be a hundred. He was a great booster for Elko, and a great booster for Nevada.

When Newt Crumley built the Ranch Inn Motel, probably one of the finest motels west of the Mississippi, we formed a men's club, like the Prospectors Club in Reno. We named it the Oreana Club, and we had lunches and special occasions. Newt had gotten the best furniture you could imagine–leather-covered card tables, beautiful leather sofas and chairs and so on. It was really high falutin'. One Christmas buffet up there, the table was about twenty-five feet long, just creaking with good food. God almighty, it was good! We realized in relatively short order, however, that Elko was small enough that a man could go home to lunch more quickly than going to a club, so it died for lack of use, basically.

When F. E. "Pete" Walters, who later moved to Reno, was still in Elko, he was the treasurer of the Oreana Club, and I was the president. A number of years ago I got a call from one of the banks, and they told me that the Oreana Club still had a bank balance. Well, we didn't have a list of names of any of the old members or anything, so I called a few of the guys I knew who had been members and asked them what to do with the money. We gave half of it to the university, I think, and half of it to the convention center or some darn thing. It was a fun place, but it just didn't get enough utilization. You know, doctors rarely spend a long noon hour drinking martinis, as some professional people are able to do, so it didn't have enough steady enough business to keep it going.

(Another activity that I have been involved in is the Rotary Club, which has been a vibrant force in my life for many years. I joined the Rotary over forty years ago, I guess, and there is only one member of the Elko club who was a member before I was.)

For many years, duck hunting was one of my greatest joys. I could tell you in July how many hours it was until the duck season opened in October. There was a gang of ten or twelve of us who would go out to the Ruby Marshes. We'd take out a bucket of stew and have stew on Thursday night and Friday. One of the fellows was a good camp cook, so we'd get hotcakes and bacon, and we always had coffee. Sometimes the fellows would play poker at night, penny-ante stuff. Some of them were pretty good poker players, and I wasn't; I didn't have enough money to play even penny-ante poker. The duck hunting was always fantastic on opening day.

Ten of us went together and bought a building that had been disassembled at the Tonopah Army Air Base. The fellow who sold it to us said that they had put it up in half a day. Well, five of us went out there to our site in the Ruby Marshes and worked all day, and we didn't get even the foundation laid, so we had to hire somebody to put it up. We didn't know what to call it until one hunting season when we were loading our stuff into a duck boat, and some other fellows came by and needed a boat ride. After we all got in the boat, we had maybe two inches of freeboard left. I asked them, "Is my gun here?"

"Yep!" they answered.

When we got out to the point to hunt, my gun wasn't in the boat; it had been left in the back of a station wagon. So they named it the "Gunless Duck Club". Fortunately, Dr. Steve Comish, a dentist friend of mine, had an extra gun. He was a terrific shot. (One opening day he was really cussing himself out because he only got twelve birds with thirteen shots.)

Our cabin was out there at what's now called Shantytown in the Ruby Marshes. Later, after some of the fellows died off, we sold it, and the man who bought it spent twenty-five or thirty thousand dollars fixing up the old cabin. I don't know who owns it now.

I went elk hunting up in Wyoming a few times with Dr. Bob Dyar from Minnesota, who was a couple of years ahead of me in medical school. Those hunting trips were always a joy. We hunted up by Dubois, Wyoming, on the east side of the continental divide. We went up over the continental divide, and I shot two or three elk over the years. Bob Dyar would get one almost every year. One year we had a moose permit, and he said, "Now if you see one, let me shoot first." The guide and I saw a moose through the trees. It had big moose horns, but Bob couldn't see it because the shafts of light sort of camouflaged it. Finally he caught sight of it, and he shot; then all of us shot.

After the last shot, the moose ran uphill for about fifty yards, and it covered maybe one hundred and fifty yards uphill before it dropped. I had never been up close to a dead moose before. It was coated with black muck, and it smelled real bad. It took all three of us to skin the side that was up; then it took all three of us to turn him over to skin the other side. We needed one pack horse for the head and hide, and two pack horses for the quarters of meat, and it was fifteen miles back to camp, which is a long ride. That was a memorable incident.

We used to have an excellent chukar population in Elko County. That is hard hunting, and I haven't done it for a long time. One time I shot a chukar, carefully marked where it fell in the sagebrush, went up there (we didn't have a dog), rested my gun against the sagebrush and started searching for the bird. I couldn't find the chukar; walking in widening circles, you know, I just couldn't find it. Then I came back, and there it was about six inches from the butt of my gun. It was so well camouflaged that I really hadn't seen it.

As for other recreation . . . for me, softball was an occasional thing,[†] but softball games used to draw big audiences, and the competition was fun. I did play tennis, and we had volleyball competitions. The doctors and lawyers were always competitors on the volleyball court, but that has changed over the years.

I used to golf and before we had a golf course here in Elko, I'd play once a year either in St. Paul or San Francisco. Tom Hood and I were the first paying customers when Elko's first golf course with grass greens opened. We had planned to play early in the morning of opening day, because it would be cooler then, but I had an OB about five o'clock in the morning, and she delivered at about six. Tom Hood was around the hospital, so I

[†] Dr. Moren was instrumental in organizing Little League baseball in Elko.

said to him, "Let's go play a round now." So we were the first golfers on the first grass-green golf course in Elko.

When we moved to Elko, old Grammar School Number One was right across the street from our house. At that time every school had its own school board, and the principal came over to our house one afternoon and said, "We need somebody to run for the school board. We had three good men on it before, and I think if I can get you to be a candidate, I can get two other guys to run." In 1947 they elected me to the school board.

When I was newly elected to the grammar school board I was condemned, because one of the first things we did was raise the salary of certified grammar school teachers with baccalaureate degrees to $4,000 a year. People thought that we were being extravagant to pay teachers that much money–that we were money-wasting buzzards. We got several bond issues passed in Elko County, including one to remodel Grammar School Number Two for $400,000. I remember that because when those bonds were finally sold, each school board member had to sign four hundred $1,000 bonds. We got fifty or sixty bids on the construction, I think, which at that time was unheard of.

I stayed on the grammar school board until Nevada changed its laws coincident with the adoption of the sales tax in 1955. Elko county became one unified school district at that time, but before that, they had over thirty school districts in Elko county! Those were interesting times. We were damned for closing up the rural schools, but we had to close them, not because it cost more money, but because you couldn't get teachers to go to one-room schools. The folks in Lamoille were really angry at me when their little school was closed.

One time a few weeks before school was ready to open in the fall, the principal came over and said, "We can't find a kindergarten teacher."

I asked him, "Have you tried Miss Wood's School in Minneapolis?" He said that he had never heard of it before, and I told him, "Well, one time I went to a football bonfire rally in Minneapolis (Clarence 'Biggie' Munn, the All-American football player, was kicking the football into the crowd.) I met this cute little girl, about five feet tall, who was a student at Miss Wood's School for Kindergarten Teachers. Why don't you give them a call?" I gave the principal the name of the place, and he called there. The girl that I met in Minneapolis agreed to come out to Elko and teach kindergarten. She stayed in Elko, and later married and had children.

In 1958, when I was president of the board, we put out a plea for a bond issue on the ballot. We had hired as our county school superintendent a man from Texas who was an excellent man, but not very popular. We had put up a bond issue for $1.5 million, and because of my unpopularity, the superintendent's unpopularity, and the bond issue's unpopularity, I was defeated and the bond issue was defeated. They passed it a year later, except that the $1.5 million bond had been increased to $2.04 million by that time to accomplish exactly the same thing. One of the things that the voters bitched about was that we hired some consultants from Stanford to help us. (This was a new experience for us, having a county-wide district, you know.)

We always had good schools, and Elko County was rated high in the state and out of state. New students who came to Elko from other schools many times were a year behind the Elko kids. That isn't quite so true now, since we've had such a big influx of children of miners. Many of them have not been in the Elko district schools long enough to become inculcated with the idea of what you can do with an education.

We started a community college in Elko, the first one in the state, I think . . . . There were a bunch of us here that got together and decided, "Well, let's get going." We were just about belly up financially when Governor Paul Laxalt came to a joint luncheon meeting of the Rotary Club, the Lion's Club, and the Women's Club. Paul announced that Howard Hughes had given a $125,000 grant to the Elko community college, and $125,000 to Nevada for a feasibility study of other community colleges. Of course, that was greeted with great enthusiasm. This was the first community college in the state, and a bunch of us had worked on it for some time. We felt that the concept of teaching people where they lived, and providing educational opportunities that didn't require a degree or necessarily work toward a degree was an important part of education.

I was a Lutheran before I got married, so I went to the Lutheran church for a while, but I didn't really care whether I went to church or not. My wife was raised as an Episcopalian, so she converted me. When the kids got old enough to go to Sunday school, I remembered that my dad said you don't send your children to Sunday school, you take them. Our church became a real important part of Laurena's life (she sang in the choir, and she became the organist); therefore, it became an important part of my life as well. We would have church picnics, and members of the church would get together for social events at the parish hall and individual homes. The Episcopalians are said to be the upper crust, and the upper crust is a bunch of crumbs held together by dough! [laughter]

There are churches of most dominations in Elko, but I have never felt or known of any religious intolerance by any one group for another, or downgrading of one group by another. There are Roman Catholics, Episcopalians, Presbyterians, Lutherans, Seventh-Day Adventists, Baptists, Jehovah's Witnesses . . . and there is a big Mormon population, maybe the biggest group in town. They are building a new Mormon church here in Elko now, and they've got one that's only a couple of years old. The Mormon group is increasing in membership all of the time, and I think that they are generally hard-working, honest people.

You've got some bad apples in every group, but I never felt anger or hostility by one group toward another.

Laurena was a member of the hospital auxiliary–they are so much help to the hospital. The Elko Hospital Auxiliary is not necessarily made up of doctors' wives; in fact the majority of them are not doctors' wives. Gosh, they have contributed a lot of money for equipment and stuff for the hospital, and Laurena was always proud of that. She was also real proud of the Nevada State Medical Auxiliary, and she and Naomi Sande and Peg Maclean were behind trying to keep that going. Laurena was sort of the herd driver, I think. She'd get on the phone and run and get them organized.

Laurena was on the board of a group in Elko to promote the idea of an auditorium and convention center in Elko. They got a bond issue for its construction on the ballot, and it was narrowly defeated. This group kept working, and when it came up for a vote again they proposed a bond issue for formation of a convention district which included Spring Creek, Lamoille, and Elko. They finally got it passed and built it, I think, in about 1970. Laurena was interested in going over the design with the architects. She convinced them that both the women's and men's toilets should have two doors–one to go in and one to come out, so that you are not trapped with people trying to go both directions through the same door at the same time. It was the first that the architects had tried that idea, and it worked out very well.

Although Laurena knew absolutely nothing about the financial management of the convention center, she had creative ideas and good judgment about functions that they could use it for. The building has served many purposes, but it was Laurena's interest in music that prompted her to get involved in the project. For a number of years before this building there wasn't any place where you could hold a concert. We used to use the old high school gym, which had been built in 1920 or something like that, but that building burned down, and for a number of years we didn't have a place with a stage. This, of course, was one of Laurena's interests, and she worked hard and did a yeoman's job in getting the community to support the project. Not all of them were behind it, and some are not even now. But the convention center has begun to make money; it's getting to be in the black in the past three or four years.

Laurena spearheaded a campaign and got a Steinway piano for the auditorium. She had hoped we could have an orchestra pit in front of the stage, but that would have cost an extra $25,000, and they couldn't afford to do that, so it was never done. The acoustics in the theater are excellent, and there are good chairs and folding tables. They can have a sit-down dinner for over six hundred people, and they have the kitchen equipment to do it. When they put on a big dinner, or something like that, they usually hire somebody either locally or from Salt Lake to cater it and cook the meals and serve them. But we have all of the equipment needed for that kind of crowd.

They hold the annual cowboy poetry doings at the convention center. There are five rooms in there that can be closed off separately with sliding doors, and at the cowboy poetry thing all of the rooms are jam-packed. The performance in front of the audience in the evening is always in the auditorium. They have been real hilarious, real fun, and well attended—not only by buckaroos, but by all kinds of folks. It is just good humor, sometimes poignant poetry, but always fun to attend. It is fun to see all of your friends, and it is sort of like going to a fair. Basically the cowboy poetry gathering evolved because of the tradition of entertainment that Newt Crumley had established through the Commercial Hotel. The cowboy poetry meeting is certainly good for the community, and certainly well received by the local population.

Laurena resigned from the convention center board in, I think, 1984. They gave her a plaque in appreciation for all her work. After her death in 1987, they named the theater the

Laurena Moren Theater. Of course, she would be as proud as punch about that.

We used to have music concerts in Elko, but they had to stop them when the old gym burned down, until they got the new convention center. Laurena belonged to the Community Concert organization which sponsored many of the concerts. She also belonged to the PEO women's group.[†] It is sort of a secret sisterhood, and they help support Cottey College, a two-year girls' school in Missouri. It is an excellent school, a good facility with a low teacher-to-pupil ratio. I have known several girls from Elko who have gone there, and they think they had an excellent education there. Laurena was a member of the PEO for many years, and our oldest daughter, Ann, was state president a number of years ago. Our other daughter, Kristin, is now state president of the organization in Utah.

The ladies in Elko also had a little Exemplar group that was sort of a study club. (They had a Christmas party every year.) It gradually shrunk, and I think there are only eight members left–there is only one husband still alive from that bunch. There were also bridge clubs all over town. My wife was not a very good bridge player; nor am I. We did play some bridge, but not very much, because we were not able to compete with the real bridge sharks.

My wife played the piano and the organ, and she'd play at church and for some of the shindigs. For a while she taught beginning piano students, just because there weren't enough piano teachers. She felt that the children should at least have a chance to learn to play the piano. One time she and a kindergarten teacher got together . . . Laurena knew how to speak French fairly well–she spent a summer in France around

---

[†] The Philanthropic Educational Organization is a women's organization that specializes in projects related to education. This rather exclusive group has been in existence for many years, and recently has become international in scope.

1933 or 1934 when she was going to a girls' boarding school in Salt Lake City–so she would go across the street to the kindergarten once a week or so and teach French to the children. The school administration found out she was an uncertified teacher and not eligible for a teaching certificate, and, even though she was teaching for nothing, they made her quit. She and the kindergarten teacher were really angry and disgusted over that, but that's the way things are. Long after she quit teaching French, people would see her in the grocery store and say, "*Oh, bon jour, Madame Moren.*" She'd get a big kick out of that.

We had a cabin out in Lamoille that we bought in 1954, and we would take our kids out there in the summertime. My wife loved Lamoille, and I had been assured many times that the children would rather go to Lamoille than see other parts of Elko County. After we got a paved highway out there, it was only twenty minutes away from home. The cabin was just a fun place to relax, and a fun place to be. After they got telephone service out to Lamoille with a private line, I could go out there, be on call, and drive back into town in twenty minutes if I was needed. They had party line telephones before that, but I didn't feel comfortable about having people listening in on my conversations with my patients.

After we got the private telephone it was great for our children and for Laurena, for I could spend a lot more time out there. The kids would go fishing and wading in the creek, play volleyball, go up the Lamoille Canyon and hike around, as well as visit with friends that also lived in Lamoille. There was a lot of family-to-family social life there. We always felt that we could enjoy life out there, but naturally there were many things we just couldn't afford to attempt, money-wise or time-wise.

Ann is our oldest child. Her husband, Bill Nisbet, is a surveyor with Chilton Engineering in Elko, and they have two boys. Our next child, Allen, works in the purchasing department of a steel forging company in Tacoma, Washington. He and his wife have two children, a boy and a girl.

Kristin, our next child, lives in Salt Lake City. She is in the financial management of an outfit that's partly university and partly privately owned. They developed a robotic arm and robots for deep sea exploration, and so on. Her husband, Tim, was a public relations man for the hospital up there, but quit to go back to college. They have a daughter, Kirin, who is recovering from being struck by a car while jogging last year. She is interested in going to medical school, and I have encouraged her to do it if she wants to.

Jim, the youngest of the family (born in 1949), is a family practice physician up in Bellingham, Washington. He was in the charter class at the University of Nevada School of Medicine when it was a two-year school. He spent his last two years at Emory University in Atlanta, where he got his M.D. Jim married a nurse, Karen Isbell, when he was a senior medical student, and they have an adopted daughter.

Some time back I asked Jim, and he said that I never put any pressure on him to go into medicine, but I am sure he knew that I would be happy if he did. I always tried not to make him hold an opinion one way or another, but it didn't work. He would do almost anything just to please me.

8

MEDICAL POLITICS

I N 1950 VAIL PITTMAN, the governor of Nevada, appointed me to the state board of medical examiners to replace Dr. Roantree, who had died. Charles Russell, who succeeded Pittman as governor, reappointed me for two terms; Grant Sawyer kept me on the board during his tenure, and so did Paul Laxalt. After that, Mike O'Callaghan appointed me for his first term as governor, but he didn't reappoint me for his second. I was on the board for twenty-seven years. Only Kenny Maclean was on the board longer than me. (He was appointed about six months before I was, and served for another year or two after I was replaced.)

The board met a minimum of four times a year–in June, September, December, and March. We used to meet in George Ross's office in Carson City. Every noon the fire whistle would go off, and Kenny Maclean would jump a foot off his chair and scare the daylights out of the rest of us. Sometime later we began to have the board meetings up on the second floor of the Riverside Hotel.

At first we didn't have very many candidates to screen, but as time went on there were more and more. Although the meetings were always too time-consuming, they were meaningful to me, because we weren't trying to keep good people out; we were just trying to identify the physicians who might be bad apples. Not always could you believe what was written in letters of reference, because no one wanted to give a potential candidate a bad recommendation in writing. We learned to make telephone calls to the state board where the applicant was previously licensed, or even pick a doctor's name from where the candidate had been practicing, and call him. Sometimes we'd find out information that could never be written on paper.

Many times we'd hold hearings and end up sort of plea bargaining: we'd revoke a guy's license once we got a complaint about him, and he or she would move on. (Most of them were men.) We had one candidate, a young man, and on the basis of a phone call to someplace in California we were told, "Oh, you'd better check with the California board; he's wanted in California for practicing without a license." We called them, and that was right. He was also being sued by three car companies, because he had leased three cars at the same time without paying the dealer anything. He had also hired several people and had never paid them. I was president of the board when he came before it, and I said, "We have some information that you owe some money in California and you're under license suspension there."

He said, "Well, that's all been taken care of."

Our answer was, "We won't give you a license now, but we'll try to do some more checking. Come back in six months."

Of course, he never came back.

We had a surgeon from Oregon who said that he had been chief of staff of a hospital, I think in Portland. All the paperwork was proper, so we licensed him, and he started a practice in Las Vegas. The Clark County Medical Society did some checking on their own, and they called, and were quite angry with us. They said, "This guy should never have been given a license." The people in Oregon had given him a good report from the hospital where he was chief of staff just to get rid of him. Then he was going to sue the Clark County Medical Society for not accepting him into its membership, which has nothing to do with his license. We missed the boat on that one.

We also missed on one of my classmates, who was licensed in Montana, I think. After giving him a license, we got word-of-mouth information that he had been in trouble in Montana for some sort of a drug problem. I sure wish we had found that out before we gave him a Nevada license. Later he worked as a prison physician, and then he worked as a physician on board cruise ships. Actually, he was well trained and a good guy. I don't know how this could have happened to him.

The law is pretty specific about licensure, and it requires that you have graduated from an accredited medical school in the United States or Canada. One applicant who had gone to a school that wasn't accredited was a friend of some people in Wells, and he wanted to practice there. A man from Wells called me while the legislature was in session, and he said he wanted to present a bill to bypass the board of medical examiners. This bill would have authorized the state legislature to grant a license. I said that basically that was wrong, and I was angry as the dickens! Well, the assembly and the senate passed the bill, but Charlie Russell, who was then governor, vetoed it.

Dr. Ernie Mack, the neurosurgeon from Reno who had helped finance Charlie Russell's candidacy, went back east and began to get some information. This guy who wanted to go to Wells had gone to school in Kansas City to something like the "Kansas City Eclectic Medical College." I wrote to the Chamber of Commerce there and got a booklet of that college's advertising for students. It had *never* been an accredited school. I sent a copy of the booklet, which listed staff members and faculty, to the AMA in Chicago, and got a letter back from one of the fellows from the AMA–"We are glad to get this information, because every one of the faculty members has been in some kind of legal trouble wherever they have been." The guy never did get a Nevada license.

Years ago we had one man who had gone to school in Hitler's Germany. He had a contact man in Berkeley, California, and he was doing illegal abortions on college gals. This was long before the Supreme Court decision on *Roe* v. *Wade*. (Then the feds found out that he didn't declare all his income with the IRS, and that he had bought two different brand-new cars that year–he had paid cash for them.) He had stated on his license application that he had graduated from a school in Germany. Nevada law didn't permit using false information on an application, so we asked the Washoe County district attorney's office to charge him with falsifying a legal document. He was convicted. (By that time, we had also gotten a list of patients on whom he had done abortions.) He appealed the conviction, and he wanted the state supreme court to have us withhold our license revocation until the case was decided. The court heard our case, and the judge made the statement that "This state board not only has a right, but it also has the duty to revoke a license for unprofessional conduct, whatever it might be."

When I was on the board of examiners one of my classmates from Minnesota came by to see me. I had learned by the grapevine previously that he was in trouble with his license in Minnesota from drugs–either taking them or selling them or whatever–and that he had his license revoked. He had come by to see me because he knew that I was on the Nevada board. He said, "Can you get me a license for Nevada?"

I said, "I'm just one member of the board. I think you are going to have one hell of a time getting a license in Nevada with that history of drug abuse."

"Well, screw you. I'll have Melvin Belli sue you." (Belli is the malpractice lawyer from San Francisco.) I learned later that he didn't sue us because he needed $10,000 up front for the lawyer; he was not able to pay it.

Drugs can be a problem for doctors. A classmate of a Reno doctor came down from Tahoe to see him one time–the guy had tried to inject himself with Demerol from one of those little glass vials, but he had broken the top and squeezed a sliver of glass into his buttocks. He got into a bleeder and couldn't stop the bleeding, so he came down, and Kenny Maclean had to stop the bleeding for the man, and he did fine. The Reno doctor's good friend had become a Demerol addict.

It is relatively easy to get the board to agree on license revocation if there is a conviction on a felony. One doctor hired a young man to drive his car down to Mexico, and he gave him $15,000 to buy marijuana, which was supposed to be worth $300,000 back here. The doctor was caught and convicted. We revoked his license for that, because a felony conviction is *prima facie* evidence of unprofessional conduct.

We had a hearing on a charge of unprofessional conduct against a physician that I knew in Carson City. It was a two-day hearing, and he came to the meeting with a briefcase full of amphetamines–it was a horrible thing. He fired his attorney and was going to defend himself. It was just like watching a man jump over a cliff; he went completely bananas. We called in a district judge to interview and observe him, and the judge agreed that the man was psychologically ill, so on that basis we revoked his license. We found out he'd been using drugs and alcohol and whatever else, I don't know. He had been a well-trained physician, and I think at one time he practiced good medicine. (He was lazy, but I think he practiced good medicine.) It was a sad thing to see happen, and he died within a few years.

Unprofessional conduct is one thing, but it is tougher than a cob to revoke a doctor's license on the basis of poor medical procedures. You've sure got to have a lot of evidence to prove that a physician is not practicing medicine according to accepted modern standards. In that respect, the board has always opposed naturopathy, or any other "healing art" having a separate licensing board, and we had a basic science law in Nevada up

until a few years ago that required that an applicant for a license
in a healing art couldn't get one until he passed a basic science
examination. (Then the applicant took the state boards in
medical science; the basic science exam was a separate board.)

The Chinese acupuncturists and Chinese herbal medicine
people applied for a special acupuncture board for their licensure.
They had a slick publicity campaign organized out of Las Vegas,
and I heard that they spent $100,000 going around the state
showing slides and movies. The entrepreneur who was pushing
the bill was going to set up acupuncture clinics all over the state,
sort of like hamburger stands. We had acupuncturists in Elko
who practiced maybe six months and folded up. I saw some
patients that one of them had treated for arthritis, and they
didn't really think they had been helped very much. Those
people were good salesmen, though–gentle, friendly, courteous
people. They do that well. They also gave free acupuncture
treatments to some of the legislators assigned to the committee
that dealt with the bill.

John Dillon in southern California and some anesthesiologists up in Washington state and the Midwest were studying
acupuncture. They were trying to do scientific studies, and we
wanted to wait until these studies were completed and we had
some facts before making a decision. Our plea was that they
shouldn't set up a separate license board. Anecdotally, there is
no question but that some people have had pain relief with
acupuncture treatments, but our concern was that most of the
acupuncture people (and chiropractors and osteopaths) do not
have adequate training to make a diagnosis, which is sort of
fundamental if you're going to practice good medicine. Well, the
legislature disagreed with us, and would not hear us, and went
ahead and licensed them.

When the pressure came for foreign medical graduates to be
licensed in Nevada, we spent three days with our attorney down
in Las Vegas discussing a bill to be presented to the legislature
that would that permit such licensing. There were specific

guidelines, and the legislature accepted them. It is probably a good thing we did that, because they had a bill ready which would have made it possible for any foreign graduate to get a license. It is extremely difficult to be certain that a person from some foreign countries really has gone to a medical school. Also the quality of medical education might be very poor, and we couldn't find out about it. One Caribbean medical school had, I think, three thousand students in the freshman class, and they didn't have any faculty or laboratory or anything. Those students were just out of the mainstream of medical education, and yet, under the provisions of the bill, they would have been qualified for licensure here as a graduate of a school like that. Many of the foreign graduates have been good doctors, but I still see problems of language barriers for some of them, both with patient-to-doctor and doctor-to-patient communications.

Nowadays an M.D. has to have a three-year residency in an accredited residency program, and an applicant might be certified by a particular board for family practice, surgery, obstetrics-gynecology, or whatever specialty, so you can learn a lot about them fairly easily. Now all of the state boards are hooked up on a central computer, so if the person is kicked out of Nevada or disciplined, all the other states will know about their action. The new computerized system of screening procedures is much better, and the computer hookup with other state boards has saved a lot of grief. It has shortened the time that it takes to get adequate, relevant, and correct information. This is a great boon to the medical community.

When I was serving, we didn't have any lay people on the board. (I was told that when they first put lay people on the state board of medical examiners, some of them would say, "I didn't like the way that person combs his hair, and I don't think we should license him." Well, that sort of reasoning wouldn't fly.)

I was a member of the Elko County Medical Society (because there were so few of us doctors in Elko County, we all took our turns as officers), and I was elected as a delegate to the state medical association. That was interesting because I got to go to state meetings. It was at my expense, but I didn't mind that. I was elected to the board of the state medical association in 1952 or 1953, and then was elected president. Bill O'Brien was secretary, and he carried the minutes of the meetings around in his hip pocket.

The Nevada State Medical Association Educational Research Foundation got started when Dr. Bill O'Brien spearheaded a program to knock out poliomyelitis in the state–they called it "KO Polio". All across the state all of the doctors gave polio vaccines for free on one particular Sunday. (We got the vaccine free from the manufacturer.) They put out a voluntary contribution box everywhere, in case people wanted to put in fifty cents or a buck, and they collected several thousand dollars around the state. The state medical association set up the educational research foundation with the money, and it has given scholarships, such as the Peter Frandsen scholarship, to medical students ever since.

The KO Polio project was a really prodigious effort, and it worked out very well. I believe that Nevada became the first state to have over 90 percent of its population immunized against polio. There was a lot of good publicity from all of the media, the newspapers and radio.

(The last case of polio in Elko county was in 1955, shortly after the vaccine program got going. Prior to that the Washoe Medical Center was the iron lung treatment center for polio victims, and they had about ten iron lungs in use all of the time. Bill O'Brien said that the anesthesiologists would rather have a general surgeon do the tracheotomy than a EENT man, because the nose and throat man made the incision so far down in the neck that the anesthesiologist couldn't get the tracheotomy tube in. The EENT man was trying to avoid damaging the vocal cords, of course.)

In 1962 I became the Nevada delegate to the AMA house of delegates, and I remained the Nevada delegate from 1962 until 1972, and again from 1977 to 1982. Because our delegation was small, we didn't have a very effective voice in political matters, so we would usually hook up with the California delegation, which had a larger voice; but I was always a little leery of that alliance, because they were a little too far left for my thinking.

As a delegate, three times a year I would fly down to Reno in the mornings; meet with the Washoe County Medical Society at noon; fly to Clark County and meet with them in the evening; then I would fly into Salt Lake and come back home to Elko. The whole trip took about twenty-four hours. In that way the board got to meet a lot of the Nevada physicians, but it was totally at my own expense. I think the state association paid us twenty-five dollars a trip like that, and when we went to AMA meetings as delegates, they paid twenty-five dollars a day. Beyond that, delegates had to pay their own way. There was airfare and hotel costs, and the meetings were always held at the most expensive hotels . . . but they were good meetings, and I made a lot of good friends over the years. They were good experiences for me, and I realized how the AMA does speak for the majority of physicians. There are people who don't join, people who don't think the AMA is worth anything. They certainly have a right to their opinion, but I think that by and large the AMA has been a good organization.

I was a delegate to the AMA when Dr. Wesley Hall was elected president of the AMA. We Nevada doctors helped elect him. At that time there were four candidates running for president, which is the first and only time, as far as I know, that there were that many. We had a good delegation of Nevada doctors, Bill O'Brien amongst them. Bill O'Brien had made a deal with Dr. Jerry Annis from Florida, who was one of the candidates. The agreement was that after the first ballot, the candidate with the fewest votes would drop out. We made a deal with him that if he lost on the first ballot, he would try to get his delegation to vote for Wes.

The next candidate was an orthopedist named Keith Henderson, who we had met in Denver–I think he was from New Mexico–and on the second ballot we made the same kind of a deal with him. On the third ballot, then, there were just Wes and Bob Long, an OB-GYN man from Kentucky. The Kentucky State Medical Society put on a huge cocktail party for the delegates, with mint juleps served in fancy glasses which read, "Bob Long, Kentucky Medical Society" on them. They had fancy hors d'oeuvres, and it was a big affair, but Wes was elected by a majority of about ten to twenty votes on the third ballot.

Wes was not a popular president with many of the AMA hierarchy, because he always said just what he thought. In his valedictory address, when he ended his year as president, he made the statement: "We in organized medicine must make sure that what happens in the medical profession is not what happened to the teaching profession. During the last few years we have trained a surplus of teachers in the United States." He wasn't saying we had a surplus of doctors, just that we should be careful that we didn't.

About that time we had formed ten or fifteen new medical schools. One of my good friends from the rural area of Elko County asked me, "What in the Sam Hill do you guys mean? The AMA is saying we have too many doctors."

I told him, "No, Wes Hall didn't say that; all he said was that we've got to be careful not to *get* too many." Of course, to my knowledge the AMA has never tried to restrict the number of practicing physicians, or the number of physicians entering medical school, in any way, shape or form. We've done a lot of work for the accreditation of medical schools, not with the intent of decreasing the number of students, but rather trying to maintain high-quality medical education. I have always felt proud of the AMA for those stands.

The idea that the AMA is trying to limit the number of physicians that are graduated each year is still somewhat pervasive. Just last year someone wrote an article in the *Wall Street Journal* accusing the American Medical Association of trying to restrict the number of physicians. It is true that after the *Flexner Report* in 1912 on medical education in the United States, the number of medical schools dropped precipitously, but that was because a lot of them had just been diploma mills.[†] Now there's a steady increase in the number of medical schools, and each school has limited the size of its entering classes, depending on the availability of faculty, the size of laboratory facilities, and so on. But the AMA has never in any way tried to limit the number of graduating physicians. In fact, they encouraged enrollment in medical schools, and for a while they even gave a lot of good student loans to medical students. They had to quit that when the interest rates on money went up to eighteen to twenty percent. They couldn't ask students to pay that, you know.

A fellow by the name of Cooper wrote a book about the AMA a few years ago, and he said that Wes Hall, M.D., was an aberration in the history of AMA presidents. I took a little personal objection to that, but that man's entitled to his opinion. The fellow suggested that Wes was not a conformist, if you will, and not in tune with the high politicians within the AMA. My feeling was that Wes did his homework well. When he was on the AMA board of trustees, he may very well have been the only trustee who ever went over the entire nine hundred-page AMA budget, line by line. He was very concerned about expenditures.

They changed the executive vice presidency of the AMA around that time, and Wes took objection to the way they did

---

[†] The *Flexner Report* (1912) to the Carnegie Foundation on the Advancement of Teaching recommended sweeping changes in American medical training, including more rigorous certification standards.

it–sort of a punch in the nose idea. Jim Sammons, a general practitioner from Texas, became executive vice president. (Jim just resigned from that position a year or two ago under a little bit of a cloud. Apparently the AMA had guaranteed a loan for his house, or something like that . . . . I don't know all of the details.) I thought that Jim Sammons did a very credible job while he was executive vice president, but he was sort of a humorless man, and I'm sure some people didn't like him because of that. The executive vice president's position is a full-time job, and when Jim Sammons took over the job, the AMA was in real financial trouble. I think now their assets are something like $100 million.

During the time that I was a delegate to the AMA, Congress passed Medicare while Lyndon Johnson was president. They stacked the deck, really. We, as an organization, did not object to government help in funding medical care for the elderly, but we felt it should be somewhat on a means basis. In other words, a millionaire shouldn't get the same amount of public support as a pauper. This concern of the AMA was never made prominent in the news reports and discussions of the issue.

Each state held special meetings concerning the Medicare issue, and delegates from the various states went to Washington. We had a couple of special sessions around that time, and tempers got pretty hot. We were invited to testify before Wilbur Mills's committee. We each had a written statement, but they wouldn't let us talk–they just accepted our written statements–but they turned out the red carpet for the president of the United Automobile Workers and for Dr. Cohen, who was that socialist from Michigan who really authored the bill.

They took our statements, but I'm sure they just threw them away. Afterwards, I asked one of the congressmen as we were leaving, "How come we were not allowed to talk?"

He asked me, "How many physicians are in the country?"

I said, "Oh, two hundred and fifty to three hundred thousand."

He says, "There are twelve million senior citizens in the country, so you figure it out." That was about how much he cared.

The AMA medical ethics board tried to come up with a paper on abortion before *Roe* v. *Wade*. One of my good friends from Washington, D.C.–a staunch Roman Catholic–was on the commission that spent two years drawing up this position paper. It was fairly well received. It was voted on by the House, but it sure wasn't a unanimous vote: sort of the kind of law that Nevada passed. Abortion is still a big topic of discussion in politics today, and it's becoming an emotional issue entirely. (I never learned how to do an abortion. When we went to school, abortion was illegal, unethical, and immoral, so I never did learn how to do one, but I can understand both sides.)

The AMA committee on ethics proscribed advertising, except for an announcement like a two-inch by two-inch ad: "Dr. so-and-so is moving his office to such-and-such an address, telephone number, office hours by appointment . . . . " Then when the feds declared that it was legal to advertise, the AMA stand was that the advertisement must be honest; that it should not claim benefits that could not be substantiated; and that prices were usually not to be announced. (I'm not sure whether the ads could list price limits or anything.) For the new doctor coming to town, or moving, or something like that, these advertisements were all bona fide and acceptable. Ads that made obviously false claims, and claims that just couldn't be documented, were considered unethical. I am not really happy about medical advertising. Obviously, if a physician locates or relocates he certainly is welcome to announce it in the newspaper, but in a reasonable-sized ad instead of a full-page ad, and so on.

The percentage of practicing physicians who are members of the AMA hasn't increased very much over the years, but I'm still a firm believer that it's the only organization on the national political scene that can speak for physicians. The new executive vice president of the AMA is Jim Todd. Dr. Todd is a very dedicated, conservative physician who is interested in the AMA fulfilling its stated objectives honorably and honestly. Even though I am partially retired from practice, I still keep my membership in the AMA, and I'm still supporting it.

Among those who were promoting the establishment of a medical school in Nevada, Dr. Fred Anderson was perhaps the most effective. Fred was a university regent, and he served as Nevada's representative to WICHE.[†] I had very little to do with the development of the school, except trying to talk to individual legislators and trying to convince them that Nevada could support a medical school. We knew that they were expensive institutions, but it would at least open the door to more Nevada students getting admitted into medicine, because any who wanted to had had to go to medical school out of state before that. Fortunately, for many decades prior to the creation of the medical school, the University of Nevada had a fine basic science and pre-med program under the direction of Peter Frandsen.[‡] Professor Frandsen was a great man, and he was responsible for many physicians in my age group going into medical school. His program was well designed, he himself was an excellent teacher, and his reputation was outstanding. If a medical school in this country received a good recommendation from Dr. Frandsen, it knew that the applicant was going to be a good student, and Frandsen was of great service to a lot of physicians in Nevada. (The Peter Frandsen Scholarship from the Nevada State Medical

---

[†] WICHE is the acronym for the Western Interstate Commission for Higher Education. WICHE studied the facilities for medical education and the availability of physicians in Nevada, Utah and Idaho.

[‡] Peter Frandsen, a Harvard-educated biologist, was a longtime and widely respected educator in basic sciences at the University of Nevada.

Association Educational Research Foundation is named in his honor.)

In the late 1960s, when the state finally got down to the nuts and bolts of starting a medical school, there was a lot of controversy–Las Vegas versus Reno, and north versus south attitudes, but the feeling amongst those of us who were anxious to get a medical school in Nevada was that we had to have homogeneous support within the medical profession. Because the University of Nevada at Reno had the basic science courses well established, and had well-organized libraries and so on, it was felt more advisable to build the school in Reno. The first class started in 1971, and for the five years it took before it became a four-year school it seemed that Reno was the best location for the medical school. Since then, of course, Las Vegas has grown, and they have more hospitals.

Before the start of the medical school in Nevada, there were never more than ten or twelve Nevada students undergoing medical education at schools scattered around the country at any one time. After the school had been in existence for several years, we had maybe a couple of hundred Nevada students who had trained here and were now in residency programs scattered all over the country. I think that on the average they did very well in competition with those who had gone to other four-year schools to begin with.

Laurena, my wife, was on the medical school's advisory board for a while, and not just because she could write notes and so on. She was interested in the auxiliary of the state medical association, which did tremendous work to help get the school started. Everyone knows that a medical school is really a luxury as far as money is concerned, but when I think of how many students from Nevada have been able to go to medical school because we have one, who would not have had a chance otherwise, I get sort of a good feeling about the whole thing.

George Smith was the first dean of the medical school; he had been working at the Desert Research Institute before that.

George was sort of a low-key individual, not prepossessing, but he had his facts pretty well right. George was the dean when our son Jim was in the first class. One day shortly before Christmas, George called me and said, "Your son Jim is studying hard, but he is studying wrong. He goes into one sort of a subject and keeps on it for a long time. You've got to tell him that he has to study more with the broad picture in mind." I told Jim that, and he got angry with me and George both.

Then we had Tom Scully as dean for a short time. Tom is a wonderful individual, but I believe that Tom was having health problems at that time, which sort of cut down on his efficiency. He was voted by Jim's class as the outstanding teacher at the medical school. After Tom, Ernie Mazzaferri was dean for a short time. I never knew Dr. Mazzaferri very well, but I believe that he was the one who diagnosed Tom Scully's health problem correctly. He was a sharp man, an internist. Bob Daugherty has been there longer than any of the other deans and I think he has been doing a good job.[†] He is very energetic. The medical school has had problems sometimes with faculty members that are good scientists, but not very good teachers. But I think every school has some problems like that, and the University of Nevada School of Medicine has gradually gotten a reputation for treating the students and the faculty well.

After they got the medical school they had a program where the students could go out into the rural communities on rotation and work with local doctors in practice there. Our clinic was involved with that, and we have had a number of students that we worked with. I think that program has generally been good for the students and the school. It gives them an opportunity to see what one type of small-town practice is like, and get a little exposure to patient care that way.

[†] Robert M. Daugherty, Ph.D., M.D., is a graduate of the University of Kansas. He is the current dean of the University of Nevada School of Medicine.

I spent one three-year term on the admissions committee of the medical school, and after that experience I am glad that I never had to appear before an admissions committee. If I had, I probably would never have gotten to be a doctor in the first place! The admissions committee went over every candidate, and the candidates were interviewed personally by one member of the committee. Then all of the committee members were required to give an opinion as to the acceptability of that particular applicant. The committee gave their opinions with complete candor, without any sort of emotion.

The first practical nursing school in the state was in Elko. A bunch of the doctors and the hospital people got together to start it. The doctors were volunteer instructors for the LPN (licensed practical nurse) training courses. We took that job seriously, and we lectured and worked with them in the hospital. Initially some of the registered nurses sort of looked down their noses at the LPNs, but it turned out to be a life saver for our hospital. If we had not had the LPNs, many of whom became excellent nurses, we could not have kept the hospital open, for we just didn't have a big enough registered nursing staff available. We started the LPN training program some time before the Elko community college was organized, and it was not a part of the college—it was run by the hospital and the medical staff. All of the medical staff participated in trying to be teachers, instructors, and almost godparents to some of the students. Many of the students were older women and had grown children, so they weren't just kids, and they took their training program seriously and with a great sense of responsibility. It was a good thing for the medical staff, too: as the old saying goes, "A good teacher learns more about the subjects than his students."

9

REFLECTIONS ON FIVE DECADES
IN MEDICINE

P ERHAPS FEWER MEDICAL students are being taught the art of medicine now than most of us were taught in the old days. In those days the art of medicine included instilling the patient's confidence in the doctor and making the patient feel comfortable, and that was a big portion of our practice. We didn't have all the scientific advances, with miracle drugs and wonderful diagnostic procedures. Today the medical school curriculum has to be so jammed together (there is so much more to be learned, and really so little time to absorb enough of it) that the student just doesn't have the time to study the art of medicine, too. Then in practice there is often just a lack of communication between patient and physician. I think the major part of the art of medicine is listening with a sympathetic ear, giving the impression of concern and caring about the patient and the patient's family. Also, the doctor should be thinking about diagnostic possibilities that he might have overlooked with any particular individual–spending time really contemplating what is wrong with old Joe: "Have I overlooked something? Did I forget to ask the right questions?"

In ancient times when doctors really didn't have any effective therapy at all, they were still recognized as healers. I don't know if there is any mystical thing like a "healer", but I think I have had the feeling, and patients sometimes have told me, that when I come into the room it makes them feel better. I can't explain why that is—whether it is just the way that I say "good morning" or whether I smile or don't smile, frown or look worried about what is going on . . . . To a certain extent, an emphasis on personal concern and caring may account for the persistence of some of the cults in medicine, such as acupuncture, naturopathy, chiropractics and so forth, but I doubt that there has ever been any such thing as supernatural healing power.

I have seen cases where there was some sort of communication between people that couldn't be explained by the usual senses. Occasionally relatives of a patient will say, "I know this patient is not going to survive," or "I know that the patient is going to survive." They seem to have reasons that are beyond what I could recognize, but they turn out to be right. When Mother and Dad were in a nursing home in Minnesota, they were both in the same room but were separated by a curtain between them. Mother was dying of congestive heart failure, and Dad was almost totally deaf and blind, but when Mother died, he knew it right away. He said, "She's gone." How he knew that, I'll never know. I suppose it may have been some sort of extrasensory perception, but how can we be sure?

There have been instances of identical twins who were living in different parts of the country. One of them would say, "I know that my twin just died," with no apparent communication by phone or letter or anything. What there is between identical twins, I do not understand. One such twin lived here in Elko while her identical twin sister lived in Wyoming. She told me, "When I talk to her on the telephone, or she calls me, we find out that we both went out the same day and bought red purses, or gray coats, or the same kind of shoes."

It was just like they were with one another all the time. I am sure (or I guess I am sure) that there are certain empathetic feelings that between some people or between families. Whether that is true between spouses, I just don't know. I can't explain such things; any explanation would be just speculation.

If I were to give any advice to medical students today, I would caution them to be careful who they select for their role models. Consider just why you choose that individual for your role model. Is it looks? The way he dresses? His income, mannerisms? All these things are relatively superficial criteria, and that student may be disappointed. Perhaps you should consider other more worthwhile values. Secondly, the student must accept the concept that if you enter into a lifetime of medicine you will have to continue to study for the rest of your life. Any branch of medicine is going to require continuous learning. Thirdly, don't expect to get rich in the practice of medicine. You will be assured a comfortable living, but the acquisition of wealth is not a good reason for entering into the medical field. Finally, a medical student must understand that he is married to his profession, and the dictates of his practice may limit the time he is able to spend with his own family. His professional duties must take priority over his personal needs. If the medical student embodies the good characteristics of medicine and the Hippocratic oath, he should have a satisfying life.

We would have been laughed out of the hospitals if we'd come dressed like some physicians do when they come to the hospital these days. In our era, doctors didn't wear earrings, and they didn't wear their hair down to the shoulders; they dressed respectably, and didn't walk around in tennis shoes and Levis and unkempt clothing. We didn't wear expensive clothing, because none of us could afford it, but our dress was appropriate and professional, as were our demeanor and looks. There were very few full-bearded doctors in my day, and I don't recall any who had shoulder-length hair. That always looks unkempt to me. That doesn't necessarily mean that they are a bad doctors, but that sort of dress just does not add to the image of professionalism that we tried so hard to earn (and generally were able to achieve). People who called themselves doctors immediately got a certain amount of respect, and I think that contributed a lot to patient trust in the physician who was caring for them.

There are still good and caring doctors in the profession, but I think they are now relatively rare compared with the old days. Partly this is due to the development of diagnostic aids which have diminished or done away with the need for observation, the need to listen to the patient. There is no question but that the process of diagnosis has become much more sophisticated: the technology of X rays has been much improved, and provides better imaging with less hazard to the patients as well as the doctors; the laboratory has been greatly automated, speeding up lab testing and eliminating some chances of human error, and with a better understanding of physiology, more specific and more accurate laboratory tests have become available; and the development of ultrasound machines, CAT scanning, MRI machines, et cetera, has tremendously improved diagnostic capabilities.

During the five decades that I have practiced, there have been other things that have dramatically improved the quality of medicine, like prepackaged sterile intravenous solutions, disposable needles, and syringes. In surgery we now have disposable drapes and sponges, where before we had to wash them, sterilize them, and reuse them. The advent of scientific anesthesiology permitted surgical procedures that had not been possible before, and lowered the risk of all surgical procedures. The transportation of sick persons by helicopter or airplane has made it possible to move patients to sophisticated treatment centers, like burn centers and transplantation hospitals, more quickly and more safely. There used to be a big danger of fire and explosions in the operating room when we were using inflammable ether anesthesia, or later on cyclopropane anesthesia, which was very explosive. Most important of all, the development of more and better antibiotics has permitted us to treat people more effectively.

Employing such scientific and technological advances, doctors today can arrive at a diagnosis and effect a cure with perhaps greater certainty in a shorter period of time than before (even though it may cost the patient more), but this is not an unmixed blessing: it can make the physician more like someone running a factory, and I think it has been a concern both to physicians and other people. It contributes a little bit to the perception that the cost of medical care is increasing too fast, when in fact better medical care is now available than was available fifty years ago, and it is actually *worth* more. You go back to the old idea that physicians don't save lives, but they many times can help prolong lives; and they help life to be more comfortable than it used to be.

In the old days, patients didn't think of suing the doctor because they so often were friends, and they knew that they cared. I think that is less common now. Patients are being taught to shop around for doctors to find one that either they like personally or has a good reputation, or sometimes their friends will recommend a doctor. Sometimes they turn away from some very excellent physicians because someone said, "Well, he is old fashioned," or "He's an old-timer," or whatever. That is too bad, both for the patient's sake and the physician's sake.

When I first entered into the practice of medicine I never even considered the possibility of a malpractice lawsuit. When I moved back to St. Paul in 1940 and opened my own private office, my malpractice insurance was the best I could get, and coverage cost me $27.50 a year. When I tell that to patients or doctors nowadays, they laugh. I quit obstetrics about five years ago because the insurance company was going to increase my malpractice premium to about $14,000 a year, and I just couldn't afford it. I couldn't ask patients to pay for it by increasing my charges, either. We almost never heard of a malpractice suit against a physician in those early days, while now it is as commonplace as a newspaper.

The increase in malpractice suits started maybe fifteen or twenty years ago. I think that it began to increase partly because attorneys were willing to take malpractice suits primarily on a contingency basis. When they found out they could get a judgment for a million dollars or more, and the attorney could get a third or a half of that, a lot more attorneys got interested! I think that is part of the reason. The attitude amongst a certain percentage of our population seems to be, "If I can get something for nothing, why not take it?" It's like gambling or the lotteries in the various states—a certain amount of greed or desire for financial affluence makes it go.

Our entire society seems to have become more litigious, so I suppose that explains a big part of it. As you know, we have always had a small percentage of babies born that have had congenital problems or deformities, or were born prematurely. Nowadays when that happens, an attorney maintains that it's got to be the doctor's fault. It is no more the doctor's fault than the man in the moon, but if they can get some dough, they are going to go for it. I remember the days when you'd do an appendectomy and the patient would be in bed for eight days. You would get them up on the ninth day, send them home on the tenth, and occasionally you would get a pulmonary embolism that was fatal. If that happens now, it's the doctor's fault, and somebody is going to sue the heck out of him and hope to collect some big money.

It may be that the golden age of medicine is over. When we contemplate our increasingly litigious society, and when we contemplate the increase of government control over the practice of medicine, I am afraid that these factors will lead to a cookbook system of medicine. With governmental control the individual patient seems less and less important, while the averages shown by statistics become more and more important: if the average cholecystectomy patient stays in the hospital for three days, that is how long all of them will stay, no matter how they feel; if the average surgical fee for a gastrectomy is $500, that is how much the surgeon will get paid, no matter how difficult the case was. The right of the physician to make individual decisions is being limited. If that trend continues, then the golden age of medicine is truly over, and the governmental hierarchy—not the scholars and physicians—will dictate how medicine will be practiced.

Complete control of medicine by governmental agencies may occur in our country, as it has in other nations. If it does, I think that it will be devastating to many Americans, who will have to wait unconscionable lengths of time to have elective procedures done. You can't expect the physicians in a socialized system to work beyond the usual office hours, when they will get their pay checks for just putting in the standard hours. I don't think that a government-controlled system is conducive to the practice of high-quality medicine. Somebody said the other day that we would end up with a system that has the efficiency of the U.S. Postal Service and the compassion of the Internal Revenue Service. We may be in danger of developing a dual system, with proscribed government-controlled medicine for the poor people, and very expensive, high-quality medical care for the wealthy.

Certainly, in our era, nobody expected to get rich practicing medicine. I think we all expected to have a good life, but the thought of becoming millionaires from the practice of medicine never entered our heads. (Most of the physicians of my generation who are financially well off made their money in good investments, rather than from the actual practice of medicine.) When we were seniors in medical school a young physician living in Minneapolis invited three or four of us over to his house for dinner one night. He had not been in practice very long, and he had built a two-story house with stone walls that had cost him $15,000. I thought that if ever I could own a house that was worth $15,000, I'd consider myself as rich as Rockefeller. Obviously, some of the really high-production specialists of today can earn a lot more money than I ever earned or ever expected to earn, but I don't begrudge them a bit, because they can do things in medicine that I never even dreamed could be done.

We old-timers were taught that homosexuality was a psychiatric disease, and homosexuals were regarded with complete scorn. I still have extreme disapproval of homosexuality, even though I realize that many people now view it as an "alternate" life-style. The AIDS epidemic has certainly made us more aware of the medical dangers of homosexuality. In my era the thought of a couple living together without being married was anathema, and was considered to be completely immoral.

Euthanasia is another moral or ethical problem that is going to be discussed more and more. My feeling is that the job of the physician is to try to prolong useful life, where there is hope of recovering to the point of being useful. I have never been interested in ending a life. I cannot tell you how many times I have been asked, "Doc, can't you give me the black bottle?" but I could not give them something to let them die. Dr. George Collett used to say, "Sometimes people have a hard time earning release." I guess that is still a valid consideration, but I wouldn't be comfortable with approval of euthanasia. When that Dr. Kervorkian in Michigan was accused of murder by assisting with suicide, I could understand his anguish to try to relieve the suffering of those patients, but I don't want to be put in that position. When the states began to use lethal injections for execution of criminals, the AMA came out and staunchly said that no physician should be forced to administer a lethal substance.

On the other hand, I firmly believe in a living will, and have signed one for myself. I've told my children that if something happens to me so that there is no chance of recovering some semblance of useful life, they should pull the plug on the machinery. There is no question but that you can maintain a vegetable-like existence with heart and lung machines for a long, long time, and a couple of times I have been asked by a family to just let a patient die. Sometimes I have agreed that that was the best for everyone, but I didn't inject anything to cause death . . . we just pulled the patient off the respirator or whatever. That is a tough decision for the family and for the doctor, as well as for the patient himself, and I am not very enthusiastic about the wisdom of lawmakers or the courts in dealing with this kind of problem. But I guess someone has to set the guidelines.

The economics of preserving life in elderly patients, as well as in premature babies, becomes a real problem for our society. When you see a really premature infant that is sick, and you transport it to a neonatal intensive care unit, you are committing to an expenditure of up to $200,000 with no assurance that the baby is going to live or die, or be a normal child or not. If we could predict the outcome of these cases, it would be easier to make the decision, but I don't think that we have that ability yet. As far as expending our resources on elderly patients with serious health problems, I don't think that chronological age should be the criterion. Some people are old at forty years of age, and some are young at eighty, so at what age would you cut it off? Obviously this needs to be an individual decision, and it is difficult, if not impossible, to write legislation that permits decisions based on individual cases. The expenditure of our limited medical resources to do organ transplants and other such terribly expensive procedures on an individual who has other serious and life- threatening problems seems to be an irrational use of resources. But I don't know the answer. While I do not think it would be fair to ask society to ante up for a heart or lung transplant for a buzzard as old as I am, I certainly wouldn't want to deny that to another person as old or older.

There is some experimentation that suggests that transplantation of some tissue into the brain of Alzheimer patients may cause reversal or improvement of that disease. Should we use Alzheimer patients with far-advanced disease for experimentation? My feeling is that we probably should, but I would want to be pretty sure that the protocols for the experiment were carefully worked out with a multidisciplinary approach. When you talk about the ethics of euthanasia and experimentation, you have to consider religion and religious beliefs. What is important to one individual may not be important to somebody else.

I practiced medicine full time until September of 1985, when my wife Laurena underwent a modified radical mastectomy for carcinoma of the breast. The surgical specimen showed no remaining tumor cells, and all of the lymph nodes were negative for tumor. We thought that the excisional biopsy had removed all of the cancer, and I thought that she was cured. Then about Thanksgiving of 1986 I began having trouble breathing, a sort of an asthma problem. I thought that I was going to drown, and Laurena sent me up to the hospital by ambulance. I was hospitalized about three times within the month. My sisters back in Minnesota were apprehensive, and they wanted me to come back there, so I went to the Mayo Clinic in Rochester. They checked me over and said, "Yes, you have asthma," and they gave me Prednisone 60 mg. and told me to come back in three weeks. When I returned, they did a cardiac ultrasound and found that something wasn't quite right. Then they did cardiac catheterization and found that I had aortic valve problems.

Dr. Joe King at the Mayo Clinic operated on me. He found that I had a two-leafed valve, instead of the usual three-leafed one, so he removed it and replaced it with a pig valve. About ten days later I suffered a perforated diverticulum—my abdomen was as hard as a board, and I have never had such pain. I remember them wheeling me down to X ray on a gurney, and a resident leaned his elbow on my belly. He said, "Does it really hurt that much?" I think that he was trying to test me, but I thought that he had started a gasoline fire in my gut! They operated on me and I ended up with a colostomy.

When they let me out of the hospital I went back to Minneapolis to stay with my sister for a while. While I was staying at her place, some of the wire sutures that were holding my sternum together broke, and my chest clicked every time I would take a breath. There was a lot of pain, and I was losing weight, so my sister said, "You can't go on this way." They took me over to Abbott-Northwestern Hospital in Minneapolis, and Dr. Earles rewired my sternum. The cardiac rehabilitation nurse at Abbott Hospital was Karen Hime, a lovely lady who really knew her business, but I hated to see her come into the room—she would make me get up, put me in a wheelchair and take me down to the cardiac rehab room and make me exercise, and I really didn't want to exercise. She is a wonderful person, and I get a Christmas card from her every year now.

While I was still in Minnesota I learned that Laurena had recurrent metastatic carcinoma. She died in August of 1987, which was a devastating blow to me and the family. After Laurena died I decided to have the colostomy taken down, and while I was getting ready to have that done, they discovered that I had a stenotic and ulcerating carotid artery, so they did a carotid endarterectomy as well as repairing the colostomy. Then in 1989 I developed a parotitis (inflammation of the salivary gland in the cheek, the one that swells up when you have mumps). The parotid gland was full of stones and couldn't drain, and that hurt like a son of a gun. They removed the gland in March of 1989. So there was about a year and a half when I didn't care whether school kept or not. I was able to practice about half the time, wanting to do more, but just running out of steam because of my emphysema and because of pain in my back due to scoliosis, arthritis and disc degeneration. I finally had surgery on my back in Salt Lake City in May of 1991. The neurosurgeon found that I had spinal stenosis, and wasn't able to improve things very much.

For the last couple of years I have just worked in the office a couple of mornings a week. I probably will see seven or eight patients–some of them are my old patients, but occasionally I will see a new patient when the other doctors are overloaded. It is the most fun to see the patients that have been coming to see me for many years. On some of them I have a complete chart for over fifty years! I would like to do more because it is hard to keep up when you are only working part-time.

According to our clinic corporation bylaws, you cannot serve on the board after the age of sixty-five, so since 1979 I have not been on the board. They have been very good to me and I still feel a close kinship with the other doctors, although the staff has changed almost completely in the intervening years. I would like to continue to practice medicine for as long as the clinic will let me . . . it gives me a reason to get out of bed and a reason to exist.

One is sometimes asked whether he would live his life any differently if he could do it all over again. I think that I'd still go to medical school, but I might very well give more consideration to taking training in some specialty, rather than do what we called a general practice or family practice. Nowadays very few family practitioners are doing obstetrics because of the high malpractice premium costs, but for me, obstetrics was almost always the most fun part of medicine . . . but I am not so sure of that either, thinking of all the times that obstetrics took me away from being able to spend time with my family. I might choose a specialty that wasn't as totally time-consuming, day and night, holiday, weekend, whatever.

If I had my career to do over again I would certainly come back to the same area to practice; you're damn right I would!

This town has been awfully good to me. I don't ever remember hearing of Elko before I got here, but I fell in love with it, and the friends that I made early on have been friends over all of these years. I met my wife here, we raised our children here, and they went to good schools here. I couldn't think of a better career than medicine or a better place to live than Elko.

APPENDIX 1

PHYSICIANS' PROFILES

Throughout this book, physicians were mentioned without accompanying biographical information. In alphabetical order, Dr. Owen Bolstad has provided some data for many of them:

Dr. Frederick M. Anderson, a native Nevadan, graduate of the University of Nevada, and a Rhodes scholar, received his M.D. degree from Harvard University. He had postgraduate studies at both Harvard and Yale, and took a surgical residency at Peter Bent Brigham Hospital in Boston. After service in the Army Medical Corps during World War II, he began practicing surgery, first in Carson City and later in Reno. His interest in education and politics led to his election to the board of regents of the University of Nevada, involvement with WICHE, and organization of the university's school of medicine. Dr. Anderson is widely acclaimed as the father of the medical school.

Dr. Richard E. Andrews, a graduate of Stanford University School of Medicine, took a residency in radiology at Stanford prior to joining the Elko Clinic.

Dr. Eugene Bastien, a native of Illinois, was granted his M.D. degree by the University of Illinois. He spent a number of years in the U.S. Navy as a flight surgeon during the Korean War, before joining the Elko Clinic in 1955.

Dr. E. T. Bell was the longtime head of the Department of Pathology at Minnesota. Dr. Bell was best known for his investigative work regarding kidney diseases.

Dr. George Arthur Collett was born in Kansas in 1890. He graduated from Rush Medical College in Chicago in 1922 and practiced medicine in Crawfordsville, Indiana, for twenty years before moving to Elko in 1946. His son, Hugh Collett, joined the Elko Clinic in 1954, shortly after his father died unexpectedly of a heart attack.

Dr. Hugh Sherwood Collett, a native of Illinois, is son of Dr. George Arthur Collett. A graduate of Northwestern School of Medicine, he took residencies in surgery in Indiana, Pennsylvania and St. Joseph's Hospital in San Francisco. He began practicing general surgery in Elko in 1956, just six months after his father's death.

Dr. Earl LaMonte Creveling was born in New Jersey in 1886, and graduated from the Homeopathic Medical College in Philadelphia, Pennsylvania, in 1912. Licensed to practice in Nevada in 1925, he was a pioneer specialist in eye, ear, nose and throat diseases in Reno.

Dr. Paul J. Del Guidice was a native of New York, and received his M.D. from New York Medical College in 1942. He began practice in Elko in 1944.

Dr. George Fahr, a well-known internist in the Midwest, was best known for his collaboration with Einthoven in the development of the string electrocardiogram.

Dr. John S. Gaynor, a graduate of New York University School of Medicine, had surgical residencies at Bellevue Hospital in New York City and at Massachusetts General in Boston. He joined the Army Medical Corps during World War II, spending some time at Walter Reed Hospital in Washington, D.C., and some time in the Pacific theater. He practiced general surgery in Wheeling, West Virginia, until he moved to Elko in 1959.

Dr. James Noah Greear, Jr., a graduate of the University of Virginia in 1920, was one of the first well-trained ophthalmologists in Nevada. A Lieutenant Colonel in the U.S. Army Medical Corps during World War II, he began practice in Reno in 1950.

Dr. Dale Hadfield, a native of Utah, took his first two years of medical school at the University of Utah, and then graduated from the University of Louisville School of Medicine. He spent two years as a medical officer in the U.S. Navy during World War II, mostly on destroyers in the Pacific theater. He was licensed to practice in Elko, Nevada, in 1946. His wife worked in Elko as a nurse prior to their marriage, which was probably the reason that Dr. Hadfield came to Elko after the war.

Celia Hauge was dean of the University of Minnesota School of Nursing during the years that Dr. Moren was in medical school there.

Dr. Arthur J. Hood, a native of Michigan, obtained his M.D. from the University of Michigan in 1903. He was one of the progenitors of the Elko Clinic group, but retired before that partnership was formed.

Dr. Thomas Knight Hood, son of Dr. Arthur J. Hood, is a native of Elko. He obtained his M.D. degree from Washington University School of Medicine in St. Louis in 1945 and took a surgery residency at St. Joseph's Hospital in San Francisco. He practiced surgery in Elko from 1951 until his recent retirement.

Dr. Litzenburg was one of the first specialists in Obstetrics and Gynecology in the Twin Cities area, and was a professor at the University of Minnesota for many years. He was quoted as saying, "The most valuable instrument that an obstetrician could have is a big, black cigar to smoke while he is waiting for nature to take its course," a plea against needless intervention by the obstetrician during delivery.

Dr. Ernest Wood Mack was born in Reno. He received his M.D. degree from McGill University School of Medicine, and took a residency in neurosurgery at the Union Memorial Hospital in Baltimore and at the

Lahey Clinic in Boston. After service in the U.S. Marine Corps during World War II, he returned to Reno to practice. He was probably the first well-trained neurosurgeon in the state.

Dr. Kenneth Fraser Maclean, a native Nevadan, received his M.D. degree from McGill University School of Medicine. Following his internship at the University of Michigan, he stayed on to study surgery. Dr. Maclean served in the Army Medical Corps during World War II, and he began the practice of surgery in Reno in 1945. Active in medical politics and in community affairs, he was highly respected by his peers.

Dr. William Alexander O'Brien III graduated from Temple University School of Medicine. He began practice in Reno in 1947, and joined the first anesthesiology group in northern Nevada. He was active in medical politics. Dr. O'Brien died in 1991.

Dr. Alton Ochsner was a world-renowned surgeon, who for many years headed the department of surgery at the Ochsner Clinic in New Orleans, Louisiana.

Dr. Art Plank was chief of urology at the University of Iowa Medical School.

Dr. Fred McClellan Poulson was born in Utah in 1899. A graduate of New York University School of Medicine in 1925, he began practice in Elko in 1931.

Dr. John Marion Read, a native Californian, obtained his M.D. degree from Stanford Medical School. He served in the armed forces during World War II, spending some time in the Far East. After the war he took a residency in internal medicine at Stanford University. He joined the Elko Clinic in 1949 as the first board certified internist in that part of the state.

Dr. Robert Peter Roantree, a native of Iowa, graduated from Washington University School of Medicine in St. Louis, Missouri, in 1919. He was licensed to practice medicine in Nevada in 1920, and practiced medicine and surgery in Elko from that time until his death in 1950.

Dr. *Charles Edgar Secor* was born in Michigan in 1882, and was a 1905 graduate of Wisconsin College of Physicians and Surgeons, later called Marquette University. He was licensed to practice in Nevada in 1908, first in Cherry Creek and then Tuscarora. After serving in the Army Medical Corps in France during World War I, he moved to Elko and worked with partners Roantree and Hood.

Dr. *Roger Charles Seyferth* is a native of Wisconsin. He held a D.D.S. from Marquette University and an M.D. degree from McGill School of Medicine. He had a two-year residency in surgery at the Tucson Medical Center, and began practice in Elko in 1954.

Dr. *William Alger Shaw* was born in Texas in 1888, and graduated from Jefferson Medical College in Pennsylvania in 1912. He was licensed to Nevada in 1920, first practicing in Tuscarora and later in Elko. He was the first physician to do elective surgery in Elko.

Dr. *G. Arnold Stevens* received his surgical training at the University of Minnesota.

Dr. *Owen Wangensteen* was chief of the Department of Surgery at the University of Minnesota School of Medicine from 1939 to 1967. Under his leadership, Minnesota was in the forefront in the development of innovative new surgical techniques and in the training of surgeons. Wangensteen has been quoted as saying, "Tradition is great for the Notre Dame football team or for the Coldstream Guards, but it's a disaster in science because it so often represents inherited errors that are taught and passed down to generations of students without question or experimentation."

Dr. *Cecil J. Watson*, Chief of Medicine at the University of Minnesota School of Medicine for many years, was best known for his research of the metabolism of bile pigments, and his study of liver diseases.

APPENDIX 2

SOME ELKO CLINIC PARTNERS

In 1949 Jake Read (Dr. John M. Read) arrived as the first internist in Elko County, and he was the first in the clinic who knew how to read electrocardiograms. Jake's wife, whose maiden name was Peggy Peters, had been living with her family in the Philippine Islands before the war started, because her father was an executive for a Canadian insurance company in Manila. During the war they were interned in the Santo Tomas prison in Manila for four years. Peggy, who is a pretty tall girl, lost so much weight during those years that she weighed only eighty-eight pounds when she got back to the United States, and her experiences as an internee made her nervous and jumpy for a while. Although Jake's father was a well-known internist in California, and it had been planned that Jake was going to practice with him for a while, they finally decided to come to Elko. I remember the day they got into town. Jake had the trunk of his car so loaded with books that the tail end almost dragged on the ground! When Jake came here he didn't have any money, like the rest of us did, so we put him on a salary for some time. At the end of that time he became a full partner without investing any money. When Dr. Tom Hood came, we made the same arrangement.

Dr. George Moore worked with the clinic for a few years in the late 1940s, then left to practice in Hawthorne and later in Carson City.

He died a few years ago, I understand. Dr. Roantree died in 1950–his wife had died earlier, and he was living in a room at the Ranch Inn at the time of his death. He had had a gallbladder operation, so he hadn't been able to work very much for about two years prior to that. In 1953 Dr. Hadfield left to take a residency in anesthesiology. He started in Salt Lake City, then moved to Tacoma. He ended up practicing in Bremerton, Washington, until he died of a stroke five or six years ago.

George Collett's son, Hugh, came as a surgeon. He had hoped to practice with his dad, but his dad died in February, 1954, and Hugh got here in August. A Dr. Wyatt came in 1954, right after George died. He moved here for only a short time. I can't remember very much about Dr. Wyatt, for I really didn't get to know him well. Since then we have had a succession of doctors who have been here a short time. They have left for various reasons, sometimes ours and sometimes theirs.

Dr. Gene Bastien had been in the U.S. Navy during World War II, and was called back for the Korean War. He called me from Illinois and said that he'd seen an advertisement in the JAMA (*Journal of the American Medical Association*) that Ely needed a doctor. He called there, and they told him, "No. We don't need one right now. Why don't you call Les Moren in Elko?"

He called me, and I said, "Fine. Can you start tomorrow?"

Gene was a general practitioner, and he was another trustworthy man. He had done some eye examinations and refractions in the Navy, and we set it up so that he could do refractions in the clinic. There was nobody in town doing refractions at that time, not even an optometrist. He did a good job on it, too, and when we decided to build the new clinic building, we built a long, narrow room for the eye exams. He was with us from 1955 until he died of a coronary in 1968, just one month after we had moved into the new clinic building.

We had one doctor who said he was a pediatrician. We hired him for a year, sort of as a test, and he proved not to be really a good-quality pediatrician, so we let him go after the end of the year. He later died in Montana.

We finally got a radiologist in maybe 1955 or 1956, Dr. Richard Andrews. He was the first qualified radiologist in northeastern Nevada, and he upgraded the equipment and techniques immeasurably. He practiced here for a couple of years, and then he felt he could make more money in California than he could here, so he moved to Lancaster, California, and practiced there until he retired.

After Andrews left, Dr. Jim Monahan, a radiologist from Reno, came here. He had gone to school in Minnesota. Jim practiced here for a couple of years, but did not join the clinic group; then he moved to Provo, Utah. He would fly over to Elko once every week in his own twin-engine airplane to read any X-ray films that we felt should be read by a radiologist. Jim had deafness in one ear, and wore a hearing aid, but he was a real good radiologist.

Dr. George Manilla joined the clinic in about 1963, doing a general practice. He had earned a Master's degree in bacteriology before going to medical school. He was working in a pathology residency, and he went back to the University of Utah in 1970 to finish. He returned after a couple of years, and rejoined the clinic as a board-certified anatomical and clinical pathologist. He's a wonderful man—intelligent and interested in many different things.

Dr. Terry Kien came here for about ten years as a radiologist. He left a couple of years ago to go up to Montana to work for a clinic up there. It was pretty tough work, you know. There was another radiologist who came here a few years ago and soon left—he didn't last a half year. We now have a new one who took residency in Tripler Hospital in Honolulu, Dr. Joan M. Haid. She is a good radiologist, and I like her very much. She does radiology both at the clinic and the hospital, but she's a member of the clinic.

Other doctors who have joined the clinic group include Dr. Richard Matern, a general surgeon who joined the clinic in 1968. Dr. Matern served as a civilian physician in Viet Nam prior to coming to Elko. He resigned from the clinic after about five years to practice surgery in Nepal, where he has spent most of his time since leaving Elko. Dr. John D. McCarthy was an internist who was with the clinic from 1970 to 1972. Dr. Douglas Hunter, who moved to Elko in 1970 from Wyoming, is a specialist in internal medicine who was trained at Stanford University.

Dr. Darrell Bennett, who was a well-trained obstetrician and gynecologist who had trained in Phoenix, Arizona, joined the group in 1971, and then moved to Reno a year later. I liked him real well. Dr. William Fritchie, a board-certified ophthalmologist, joined the clinic in 1972. He left the group in 1975 and opened his own office in Elko. He is still practicing ophthalmology here. Dr. Howard Owen, a Mayo Clinic-trained surgeon, joined the clinic in 1972 as a general and vascular surgeon. He retired from practice in 1983. Dr. Kenneth S. Allen, who had trained at Stanford, joined the clinic in 1973 as an OB-

GYN specialist; he moved to Guam in 1984. Dr. Emmalina G. Cortez was the first board-certified pediatrician in Elko. She joined the clinic in 1975. She received her M.D. in Manila and took her residency in Baltimore.

Dr. Carlton M. Lewis joined the clinic as a family practitioner in 1976. He left the clinic in 1986 to open his own office in Elko. Dr. David M. Hogle joined the clinic in 1978. He had his medical training and residency in internal medicine at UCLA. Dr. Roy Jones joined the group in 1983. He trained at the University of Illinois, and is board certified in surgery. Dr. Richard Young trained at Johns Hopkins, with a residency in OB-GYN. He joined the clinic in 1983. Dr. S. Corbin Clark trained in urology at the Mayo Clinic and joined our clinic in 1983. He moved to Salt Lake City in 1984. Dr. Ron Bohnenkamp took a residency in pediatrics at Travis Air Force Base in California. He joined the clinic in 1983, but after one year returned to the Air Force.

Dr. Scott Denton graduated from the University of Nevada School of Medicine, took a residency in pediatrics in Tucson, and joined the clinic in 1985. Dr. Mitchell E. Miller was also a graduate of Nevada, and took a residency in internal medicine in Spokane. He joined the clinic in 1985. Dr. Christopher Ward, who took a residency in general surgery in the Air Force, joined the clinic in 1986. Dr. Rodney Handsfield, a urologist trained in Boston, joined the group in 1986.

Dr. Mike Gummer had been practicing in Battle Mountain and had sort of a loose association with the clinic, and he didn't like that; so he moved to Elko, and is solo in his own office. Dr. Roger Jones, an orthopedist trained at the Mayo Clinic, came in 1985 and joined the clinic. He was with us a couple of years, then he went on his own, and he's got his own solo practice here in Elko.

There have been quite a few other doctors that have come and gone, some after only a few months, but I just can't remember all of their names; and there were a number of doctors who practiced in Elko in the early days who were not part of the clinic group. Dr. Fred Poulson was doing general practice, and then he took ophthalmology and he practiced office ophthalmology. He did a couple of cataracts, and didn't feel comfortable doing them, so he quit doing eye surgery. Real nice gentleman. His wife Julia is a wonderful lady who has remarried, but I don't know where she lives or what her married name is now.

Dr. John Gaynor came to Elko in 1959, and practiced here until he died about ten years ago. Later Dr. Arnold Stevens joined Dr.

Gaynor, limiting his practice to surgery. Arnold Stevens had been practicing in Los Angeles, and I guess he had a fancy practice there with all the movie stars and famous people. He bought a ranch in Elko County and practiced part-time with Gaynor. He ticked me off a little bit when he said that he would be perfectly willing to help Tom Hood and Hugh Collett on some of their more difficult surgical cases, because I thought that they were better surgeons than he was. At least that was my impression. Dr. Roger Seyferth came here in 1954. He practiced alone for many years, and he retired two or three years ago.

INDEX